FOR EACH AND ALL

The Moral Witness of Asa Mahan

Christopher P. Momany

For Each and All: The Moral Witness of Asa Mahan

The General Board of Higher Education and Ministry leads and serves The United Methodist Church in the recruitment, preparation, nurture, education, and support of Christian leaders—lay and clergy—for the work of making disciples of Jesus Christ for the transformation of the world. Its vision is that a new generation of Christian leaders will commit boldly to Jesus Christ and be characterized by intellectual excellence, moral integrity, spiritual courage, and holiness of heart and life. The General Board of Higher Education and Ministry of The United Methodist Church serves as an advocate for the intellectual life of the church. The Board's mission embodies the Wesleyan tradition of commitment to the education of laypersons and ordained persons by providing access to higher education for all persons.

Wesley's Foundery Books is named for the abandoned foundery that early followers of John Wesley transformed into a church, which became the cradle of London's Methodist movement.

HIGHER EDUCATION & MINISTRY
General Board of Higher Education and Ministry
THE UNITED METHODIST CHURCH

for Kim

CONTENTS

ACKNOWLEDGMENTS

Many thanks go to a diverse collection of friends who believed in this project and who offered unconditional support and encouragement. Noelle Keller of the Shipman Library at Adrian College deserves particular mention for her kindness in locating archival materials. More than anyone may realize, the students of Adrian College have inspired me by bringing the values of Asa Mahan forward. Most of all, thank you to my son, Christopher Adam, a marvelous man who "gets" his dad and who makes me proud every day.

Introduction

ASA MAHAN, SLAVERY, AND THE MORAL LAW

In the modest Midwestern railroad town of Adrian, Michigan, students from the local college gathered on Monday night, May 15, 1865, for a meeting. This was no ordinary assembly. It represented the weekly program of the Adrian College Star Literary Society. Curriculum among nineteenth-century American colleges was fairly uniform, typically with two or three tracks of study being offered. Much was absorbed in the classroom, especially philosophy and literary classics, along with some of the emerging sciences. Yet critical learning among these schools often took place in various literary societies. Such groups served a social function, but they were really a structured part of the educational environment.

Literary societies combined prayer, the reading of essays, sometimes brief musical recitals—and most especially debate. At each meeting students would consider a formal resolution and then argue for or against the statement. They usually held a vote to record their conclusions regarding the question.

On that night the students at Adrian College filed into their assigned room; read and accepted the minutes from the previous meeting; then heard a selection of music and a speech. The address was titled "General Grant." After all, General Robert E. Lee had surrendered his Army of Northern Virginia to General Ulysses S. Grant on April 9, 1865. The Civil War was a fresh and horrifying reality. Then the group considered a resolution for debate. The statement asserted that the creation of humanity "as the ultimate design of God can be proved from Nature outside of

Revelation."[1] It was an astounding claim—some might say outlandish. The recent war had taken the lives of 620,000 people.[2] How in the world could these students consider the splendor of humanity in the wake of such slaughter? Perhaps most bewildering of all is the claim that human dignity could be discerned from nature, the world of experience.

Adrian College students were well-versed in Scripture. They held a very high view of revelation. Yet here they looked to the world around them. Their campus was removed from that period's battlefields, but these young people were not protected, nor were they naïve. Some of their friends had been horribly maimed or killed in the recent conflagration. And still, after ample discussion, "a motion for the adoption of the Resolution was made and carried."[3] Humanity: the ultimate design of God!

Any credible explanation for their conviction is conjectural, but we should not be surprised if the teaching of their beloved president, Asa Mahan, lurked behind the affirmation. Mahan was a well-traveled human rights advocate and philosopher. Later after the Civil War he set to work on a book that was released in 1867: *The Science of Natural Theology*. Here he argued that God's attributes of infinity and perfection are "penciled out" among people, the finite image of the infinite.[4] Mahan left many puzzling and inspiring treasures regarding his view of human dignity. Among them is his handwritten notebook of lecture outlines, sermon ideas, and

---

1 Star Literary Society, Constitution and Bylaws, Minutes December 16, 1859–September 18, 1867, Archives, Shipman Library, Adrian College, May 15, 1865, 248.

2 Some historians believe the number is even higher. See Guy Gugliotta, "New Estimate Raises Civil War Death Toll," *New York Times*, April 2, 2012, http://www.nytimes.com/2012/04/03/science/civil-war-toll-up-by-20-percent-in-new-estimate.html. The print version of this column appeared April 3, 2012, on Page D1 of the *New York Times*, under the title, "New Estimate Raises Civil War Death Toll."

3 Star Literary Society, Minutes, May 15, 1865, 248.

4 Asa Mahan, *The Science of Natural Theology; or, God the Unconditioned Cause, and God the Infinite and Perfect, as Revealed in Creation* (Boston: Henry Hoyt, 1867), 233.

commentary on the United States Constitution. This artifact of 281 pages was left at Adrian College following the Civil War.

By 1865 Asa Mahan was a legend—a veteran of the Underground Railroad, a philosopher, and a pastor known for his Wesleyan views on Christian Perfection. In earlier days he had been the first president of the Oberlin Collegiate Institute. Six feet in height with commanding features set off by a long gray beard, Mahan made an impression. College students loved him. He never tried to be anyone other than himself. During the 1830s he served as a pastor and member of the board at Cincinnati's Lane Theological Seminary. When students spoke against slavery, most elders opposed them, but not Mahan. He was an unqualified advocate for the young people. He knew they were right, and right meant something.

By 1835 Mahan already possessed a reputation for antislavery agitation, and he would guide the college at Oberlin for fifteen years. It was a community known for consistent and controversial reform activities. To many, Oberlin became the epitome of dangerous egalitarianism. To others, it represented a glimpse of God's kingdom on earth. Oberlin was really its own kind of place: radical by most standards but not under the control of New England abolitionists. Its theology was remarkably traditional, reflecting core Protestant identities. Yet its prophetic social stance infuriated those with power. Just what kind of ideology drove this colony of threatening zealots? Oberlin's antislavery argument reveals and conceals much at the same time. We are fortunate that Asa Mahan did not keep things to himself. He wrote much of his conviction down in that notebook of lecture outlines, sermon ideas, and political commentary.

Mahan's antislavery conviction, like that of countless others, came from his articulation of the "moral law." He was among the generation of college presidents devoted to teaching a course on moral philosophy (ethics) before graduating young leaders. Other abolitionists helped people find freedom or worked the halls of Congress without such elaborate theorizing, but many lived a witness that expressed their philosophical teaching and writing. Mahan was one of the latter.

Asa Mahan at Oberlin 1842 Oil Painting.
Photo courtesy of the Oberlin College Archives.

His personal notebook contains an especially pithy definition of the moral law. When pondering the requirements of moral law, Mahan jotted down three characteristics. First, the moral law requires a respect for all objects "according to their intrinsic worth." This brief statement is easy to overlook but it grounded Mahan's entire ethic. Things and people possess an objective value. Second, the law can be expressed in language akin to Immanuel Kant's Categorical Imperative: "So will an intent, that you may properly regard the motive from which you act as a rule to all intelligents." Third, Mahan borrowed from French philosopher Victor Cousin, who mirrored Kant by stating that right motives ought to be universal rules.[5]

---

5   Asa Mahan, "Manuscript Writings, Miscellaneous," Archives, Shipman Library, Adrian College, Page 106.

This eclectic bit of reflection could occupy sensitive minds for a long time, but Mahan added one more layer of complexity. He claimed that these three emphases were really identical and he claimed that they all conformed to the idea of moral law required by the Bible. When one gets beneath the subtleties, one finds that Mahan owed much, if not all, of his conviction regarding the moral law to Immanuel Kant. Moreover, he was willing to identify this conception with the law of God. We may or may not dispute his conclusions, but we should acknowledge his reasoning as, at least, bearing some measure of consistency.

In November 1846 Mahan published a theoretical critique of the abolitionist movement: its successes and failures. He was concerned that adherents and opponents alike gain clarity regarding the central issue at stake. Mahan revered America's revolutionary period. He knew the narrative of founding struggle—military and political figures, the chronology of battle, as well as strategy. Yet this story was meaningless without a grasp of core principles, especially the yearning for freedom. Likewise, Mahan claimed that those determined to comprehend the abolitionist movement must understand its principles. He wrote: "Every individual, for example, wholly misapprehends the antislavery movement . . . who does not contemplate it in the light of the eternal and immutable distinction between a *person* and a *thing*."[6] The difference may seem self-evident, but there was a more sophisticated logic at play.

Few would question the distinction between persons and things, and so it might seem curious, to say the least, that any abolitionist would hang such important work on the differentiation. But many did. Students of Samuel Taylor Coleridge often invoked his habit of stressing the difference between people and things. For instance, Frederick Douglass borrowed from Coleridge when he released his second autobiography. The title page read: "By a principle essential to Christianity, a PERSON is eternally differenced from a THING; so that the idea of a HUMAN BEING, necessarily excludes

---

6   Asa Mahan, "Certain Fundamental Principles, together with their Applications," *Oberlin Quarterly Review* Article 35 (November 1846): 228.

the idea of PROPERTY IN THAT BEING."[7] This appreciation for Coleridge did not automatically make Douglass a voice for Romanticism or New England Transcendentalism. His second narrative declared independence from the overweening influence of William Lloyd Garrison and other Easterners. Still, the critical distinction between persons and things touched a nerve.

Aside from common moral contemplation, was there a particular source that celebrated the difference between people and things? The answer is yes. Moreover, that source was anything but commonplace. A critical movement among Immanuel Kant's *Groundwork of the Metaphysic of Ethics* (1785) explored the very distinction in question. Many will not recall this discussion. It was embedded within Kant's signature reflection on means and ends, and one expression of the Categorical Imperative stressed that people are ends in themselves. Yet if we look again, we find that this very exploration of the tension between ends and means mirrors a conviction about the ontological difference between persons and things. When contemplating the value of inanimate realities, as opposed to beings possessed of reason, Kant wrote:

> Even those external things whereof the existence rests not on our will, but depends on nature, have, *as irrationals*, a relative value only, and are used as means and instruments for our behoof, and are therefore called THINGS; whereas an Intelligent is called a PERSON, he being by the constitution of his system distinguished as an end in himself, *i.e.*, as somewhat which may not be used as a mere mean, and as restraining to his extent the arbitrary use which other wills might make of him, and becoming, by force of such restraint, an object of reverence.[8]

Things might be a means to an end, but people are ends in themselves.

---

7   This statement is a very close paraphrase of Samuel Taylor Coleridge, "General Introduction; or, Preliminary Treatise on Method," in *Encyclopaedia Metropolitana* (London: B. Fellowes, 1818), 32.

8   Immanuel Kant, *The Metaphysic of Ethics*, trans. J. W. Semple (Edinburgh: Thomas Clark, 1836), 44.

Asa Mahan's handwritten manuscript notebook.
Photo by Hollie Smith. Courtesy Adrian College Shipman Library.

Once we trace Asa Mahan's fondness for two recognized expressions of the Categorical Imperative, we might ask whether he ever relied on other variations. This he did. Of particular importance is the German philosopher's attempt to express the Imperative in political and social terms. If people were ends in themselves, then communal, even governmental, commitments called people to respect one another among a "kingdom" or "realm" of ends. The implication for political covenants was not lost on Asa Mahan. He viewed the United States Constitution as an instrument aiming to create a national community where each and every person would be treated as an end in himself or herself. Manipulative readers might try to justify slavery by appealing to the Constitution, but the very purpose of the document, according to Mahan, could not tolerate this interpretation.

In an America where most people were either antislavery and anti-Constitution or proslavery and pro-Constitution, Asa Mahan was antislavery and pro-Constitution. This unusual perspective occupied his mind to a great degree. He devoted the last 64 pages of his 281-page personal notebook to a detailed and abolitionist commentary on the United States Constitution. The inside back cover of this artifact features Mahan's celebratory note regarding passage of the Thirteenth Amendment.

Kant and Abolition

There are several ironies involved in Immanuel Kant being considered a philosophical inspiration for the antislavery cause. On a larger scale, we might note the way in which European human-rights traditions developed during the Enlightenment. Contemporary philosophers and jurists observe that continental thinkers gave impetus to those theories that stressed communal responsibility and social welfare, whereas Anglo luminaries emphasized individual rights and freedom.[9] A careful study of the way philosophical traditions influenced the American antislavery movement reveals how continental thinkers, especially Kant, provided a universalizing framework that was employed by abolitionists to protest the sacrifice of any human being for the desires of another. In contrast, British moral philosophy would include more "utilitarian" considerations—a perspective that, in America, provided rationale for sacrificing some to advance the agendas of others.

American moral philosophy evolved along unique lines and was contextualized to explain as much as to mandate. The general trajectory of formal reflection followed two competing approaches: that of deontology and teleology. The first derived its principles from a variety of Scottish intuitionists and Kant, holding that right and wrong are inherent qualities of action. Even a desired end could not redeem immoral behavior. The opposing view argued that consequences of value determined the ethical quality of action. For this reason, teleological views are often termed "consequentialism." Of course, this teleological perspective came in many

---

9   Mary Ann Glendon, *A World Made New: Eleanor Roosevelt and the Universal Declaration of Human Rights* (New York: Random House, 2001), xvii.

forms, from relatively mild concerns for "benevolence" to rather blunt calculation of benefit found in some utilitarianism.

These two frameworks were especially important for consideration of slavery in the antebellum age. Teleological concerns and their focus on consequences seemed more flexible and adept at serving institutional ends. They also equivocated when it came to human bondage. Deontological perspectives and their grounding in inherent values left little room for compromise and were criticized for being extremist, but they served the antislavery cause well.

We should not conclude that the early shapers of these two schools intended them to serve this role in the slavery debate. Some teleological thinkers were stridently opposed to slavery, and many deontologists were not equal to the human rights demands of their theories. Immanuel Kant is a prime example.

Despite providing moral reasoning that was later adapted by many Americans to fight slavery, Kant is remembered as someone with reprehensible views on race.[10] His notoriously disrespectful comments about people of African descent in *Observations on the Feeling of the Beautiful and Sublime* (1764) cannot be explained away. If the Konigsberg philosopher became any source of guidance for American antislavery moral philosophers, it was not because his personal views stood above reproach. Rather, some abolitionists were captivated by Kant's analysis of means and ends and how that relationship reveals ontological truths regarding the worth of people.

Taken as a whole, Kant's rarefied examination of means/ends, things/people has left a compelling legacy. Within our present century, David Brion Davis wrote: "*All* forms of slavery embody a profound and inherent contradiction, illustrating the most extreme form of a tension we experience almost daily in more subtle or benign interactions of inequality. I refer to the desire to dominate another person until she or he becomes a

---

10 David Brion Davis, *Inhuman Bondage: The Rise and Fall of Slavery in the New World* (Oxford: Oxford University Press, 2006), 75.

willing extension of our own will, an instrument to serve our needs."[11] Understanding the way this dynamic was exploited among the varied forms of Atlantic slavery is critical. Even more, understanding the way this dynamic was critiqued and countered by thinkers, teachers, and writers promises hope for today's scholar/advocate.

A concern for first principles when it comes to explosive issues can be written off as meaningless. However, a demand for outcomes can be but one more expression of the will to power. Theory matters now, even as it mattered in the late eighteenth and nineteenth centuries. This investigation will take the influence of European moral philosophy on the American antislavery movement seriously. In the process, I do not claim that every effort in antebellum America to confront slavery was the result of some deliberate articulation of philosophical principles, but I do suggest that the implications of certain values, ideas, and moral reasoning played a part among the movement.

Some might conclude that the American antislavery phenomenon was driven by cultural, religious, social, economic, and racial forces that defy philosophical precision. I will not dispute the point, but I will posit that the influence of particular philosophical frameworks was more prominent than is often acknowledged. How did American thinkers and writers understand the very nature of personhood coming out of the revolutionary period, and how did those understandings reflect indebtedness to various European philosophical sources?

Beyond Interpretive Assumptions

It has not been fashionable to emphasize Kant's influence on antebellum philosophy. Most scholars presume that his impact came later, after the Civil War. This is especially the case when considering religious thinkers outside of New England. Immanuel Kant may have contributed to the rise of Transcendentalism and other northeastern American currents, but

---

11 David Brion Davis, *Challenging the Boundaries of Slavery* (Cambridge: Harvard University Press, 2003), 6.

observers assume that the Scottish philosophy of Common Sense ruled antebellum America. This appraisal is not incorrect, but it is oversimplified.

Common Sense Realism was a philosophy codified and then popularized by Thomas Reid (1710–1796), Dugald Stewart (1753–1828), and others. Many identify its establishment in America with the college presidency of John Witherspoon at Princeton (1768–1794). This perspective claimed for humanity an innate ability to know the world as it really exists. Moreover, realists of the Scottish school held that every human being enjoyed the intellectual capacity to conceptualize both the self and others with remarkable accuracy. Realism was, at once, a straightforward and explicitly egalitarian viewpoint. It was also considered an intellectually safe and moderate alternative to more inventive theories of knowledge.

Philosophical approaches never exist in a vacuum, and even these early American schools developed a regional flavor. Idealism, the philosophy that stressed our subjective perceptions, found fertile soil in New England. Materialism, the philosophy that stressed objective, verifiable facts, was especially strong in medical science. Philadelphia is remembered as the nursery for a materialism that then radiated south. Realism, with its emphasis on both faculties for knowing and trustworthy truths, was associated with the middle colonies and then with a westward movement into the Old Northwest. Immanuel Kant's metaphysics or view of reality was idealist to the core. His categories of perception placed less emphasis on the objective world, and he found a sympathetic audience in New England. But this fact does not prove all teachers and writers of the middle regions limited themselves to Scottish Realism.[12]

Asa Mahan hailed from New York State—a famed laboratory for religious innovators who tethered their movements to the certainties of Scottish Common Sense. Yet Mahan blended Scottish and Kantian insights. Writing in the early twentieth century, philosopher Charles M. Perry observed that, "Asa Mahan . . . at one time president of Oberlin College and later of Adrian, read Kant and his successors with shrewd intelligence,

---

12 See especially I. Woodbridge Riley, *American Philosophy: The Early Schools* (New York: Dodd, Mead & Company, 1907).

though after all his wandering in forbidden territory he came safely back to Scottish common sense."[13] Perry was not wrong. Asa Mahan spent his twilight years writing a two-volume magnum opus that clearly supported realism.[14] Yet suggesting that Mahan, the quintessential middle-American pastor/teacher, flirted with Kant before settling on some presumed safety of Scottish philosophy distorts the record.

In 1845, Mahan wrote among the dedicatory preface to his *Intellectual Philosophy*: "The individuals to whom I feel most indebted as a philosopher, are Coleridge, Cousin, and Kant—three luminaries of the first order in the sphere of philosophy."[15] This statement bears some unpacking.

Samuel Taylor Coleridge was received as an English interpreter of Kant, but he never shared the German's knack for systematizing. Many trace the philosophical influence of Coleridge in America to James Marsh, president at the University of Vermont. Marsh introduced Coleridge's *Aids to Reflection* in 1829 and gave it enthusiastic endorsement.[16] Victor Cousin was a French philosopher and founder of the school known as "Eclecticism." He was celebrated for his ambitious attempt to integrate Kant and the Scottish realists. In many respects, Cousin's thought set a pattern for Asa Mahan. Here was a French thinker who appreciated experience, as did most English-speaking philosophers. Yet Cousin saw experience as an indicator of transcendent, universal truths (something emphasized by the Germans). It is worth noting that Oberlin College required its students to engage in close study of Cousin. The 1836 catalogue at Oberlin lists Cousin's *Elements of Psychology* as required reading, along with the work of Scotland's Dugald Stewart.[17]

---

13 Charles M. Perry, *Henry Philip Tappan: Philosopher and University President* (Ann Arbor: University of Michigan Press, 1933), 108.

14 Asa Mahan, *A Critical History of Philosophy*, 2 vols. (London: Elliot Stock, 1883).

15 Asa Mahan, *A System of Intellectual Philosophy* (New York: Saxton & Miles, 1845), iii–iv.

16 Bruce Kuklick, *Churchmen and Philosophers: From Jonathan Edwards to John Dewey* (New Haven: Yale University Press, 1985), 121–22.

17 *Catalogue of the Trustees, Officers, & Students of the Oberlin Collegiate Institute, Oberlin, 1836* (Cleveland: F. B. Penniman, Book and Job Printer, 1836), 22.

Asa Mahan at Adrian College.
Courtesy of Adrian College Shipman Library.

Immanuel Kant's direct influence on mainstream American higher education received a boost from the 1836 translation of his ethical theory by J. W. Semple, a Scot. Asa Mahan's 1848 *Science of Moral Philosophy* includes lengthy quotes from Kant that appear to be excerpts of Semple's rendering, and it is no surprise that much of the material quoted refers to the Categorical Imperative.[18] None of this is to say that Immanuel Kant's thought dominated the Old Northwest before the Civil War, but the evidence suggests that his influence was more pervasive than many acknowledge.

Instead of concluding that Asa Mahan and perhaps others like him toyed with Kant before settling on more acceptable Scottish concepts, we

---

18 See for instance Asa Mahan, *Science of Moral Philosophy* (Oberlin, Ohio: James M. Fitch, 1848), 268–69.

ought to consider a different interpretation. Early American philosophy made very explicit distinction between its approaches to reality (metaphysics and epistemology) and ethics (moral philosophy). Some who remained essentially realists in their truth-claims embraced Kant's moral principle. This was especially true when comparing deontological and teleological ethical values. Britain's William Paley promoted a teleological view that calculated morality according to measurable consequences, and Asa Mahan resisted this approach throughout his career. Very near the end of his life, Mahan had this to say: "While we differ totally from Kant in the sphere of Philosophy [metaphysics], we are compelled to regard him as a far more correct and safer expounder of moral principles than Paley."[19] It was possible to appreciate Scottish notions of certainty while employing and deploying Kant's Categorical Imperative.

A World of Ideas and Experience

This book is not a biography. It does not pretend to cover every aspect of Asa Mahan's life, and it concludes its exploration at the end of the Civil War. It *is* an attempt to trace powerful ideas in the teaching and writing of ethics through the Civil War, and it asks how these ideas were embodied among the debate over slavery in America. Asa Mahan's life serves as a lens through which to view the interaction and sometimes the outright mutual exclusivity of these ideas.

Today it is easy to segregate ourselves within disciplines and even to separate ourselves from the world of ideas. An ordained clergyperson who articulates the finer points of philosophy is rare, and those dedicated to studying American intellectual currents are not typically representatives of organized religious movements. Asa Mahan was both a pastor and student of profound ideas. He is perhaps best known for his theological contributions to the tradition that advocated Christian Perfection or Holiness, but these practices of faith were informed by his philosophical acumen.

---

19 Asa Mahan, *A Critical History of Philosophy*, Vol. 1 (London: Elliot Stock, 1883), 280.

Mahan lived during an era when there was more crossing of boundaries, at least the boundaries of academic specialization and theological vocation. He was also an engaged citizen. He typified a period when those who read philosophy were not necessarily removed from day-to-day concerns, and those who advocated change did not look on thought with disdain. Race, gender, and class (among other identifying factors) kept people apart. But doers were often thinkers, and thinkers were often doers. We might write off the lives of those who read and wrote and taught in antebellum America as guardians of privilege, and some deserve this judgment. Many do not. Asa Mahan and several others knew what it meant to work the land, interact with a wide range of people, and manage small enterprises. They also knew that their thinking and writing required sacrifice to make a more just world.

Mahan's experience during the Civil War years epitomized these integrated qualities. While defending arguments in metaphysics and moral philosophy, he also made time to run a college that was open to all—women and men, as well as people of color. He worked with African American intellectuals, such as physician and Civil War medical officer Martin Delaney, and he was trusted by daughters and sons of the enslaved. Once safely in Canada, some families sent their children back across the border to study with Mahan. During the war Asa Mahan traveled to Washington, DC, and advised Abraham Lincoln regarding military strategy. He was an advocate for economic aid at home and for freed people following the conflict. Perhaps most of all, this person of almost unimaginable intellectual energy paid a price in personal grief for his commitments and the commitments of his family.

Asa Mahan's son Theodore died from wounds received in front of the stone wall on Marye's Heights at the Battle of Fredericksburg. Anyone who has walked that killing ground will shudder at the audaciousness of those willing to storm such an impregnable place. Mary Mahan, Asa's life-partner, also died during the war, as did their daughter, Elizabeth. President Mahan excelled at abstract arguments, but his life was no abstraction. We have much to learn from him today about faith, thought, and the labyrinths of philosophy. We also have much to learn from him about what it means to be a citizen and a survivor in times of social and personal grief.

This determination and steadfastness is perhaps best illustrated by Mahan's unyielding dedication to constitutional government. Despite bearing the scars of conflict and hatred, he refused to give up on the notion of a better nation. Some might bend national aims to their self-interested agendas, and others may walk away from the bonds of civil covenant in exasperation. Not Asa Mahan. His citizenship, like his thought, had staying power.

So we might as well let go of preconceived notions that a study of this nature is all about philosophy or all about a "good story"—about scholarship or drama—about religious movements or secular commitments to each other. It is about all of these things—and more. Today's thinkers who are also doers and doers who are also thinkers will not bring back yesterday. Thank goodness. There is much about the past that we need not repeat. Yet those who managed to integrate a collection of critical concerns can help us avoid isolating ourselves, especially when both deep thought and comprehensive care are needed. That is why this study has something to say to us.

One

THE RIGHT
AND THE GOOD

A Distinction between "Is" and "Ought"

The year 1859 was memorable, and memories can have mixed qualities. The United States stared into the abyss of Civil War, and the meaning of this impending conflict harbored as much angst as the war itself. Today we recall October 1859 as the time John Brown and a ragtag group of armed antislavery people took Harpers Ferry, Virginia (now West Virginia), by storm. Brown's hope for a larger insurrection among the enslaved failed miserably, and over the years he has been judged an imbalanced advocate, at best—a bloodthirsty breaker of laws, at worst.

Yet 1859 also marked a lesser-known event of civil disturbance. That winter and spring, some months before Brown's raid, a collection of citizens from Oberlin, Ohio, and nearby Wellington, thirty-seven in all, stood trial in federal court. Their crime: they had openly violated the government's so-called "Fugitive Slave" legislation of 1850.[1]

According to most recollection, a young man named John Price escaped slavery in Kentucky and lived in northern Ohio for some years. During the late summer of 1858 kidnappers were sent to seize him. Price was abducted outside of Oberlin and taken to the town of Wellington, where the captors planned to spirit their prisoner away by train. Before

---

1 The story, including detailed records of court proceedings, was originally published in Jacob R. Shipherd, *History of the Oberlin-Wellington Rescue* (Boston: John P. Jewett, 1859). Several other accounts have appeared over the years.

they could leave town, the posse of kidnappers was spotted, and citizens from both Oberlin and Wellington rallied to save the young man. Several hundred gathered near a hotel where the kidnappers and prisoner waited for the next train. The crowd of antislavery people grew, and finally someone forced a way into the hotel and the room where John Price was held. The "rescuers" got him safely into a buggy and headed back to Oberlin, where he was protected until such time as he could move further north to permanent freedom.

Resentment against the Oberlin-Wellington "rescuers" simmered until a federal grand jury of the Circuit Court for the Northern District of Ohio indicted those who freed Price. The rescuers were charged with violating the Fugitive Slave Law of 1850, a federal law designed to facilitate the capture of those escaping slavery. The trial unfolded during the early months of 1859. Witnesses were called to document events, and attorneys used the opportunity to argue either for or against the 1850 legislation. It was obvious that more was on trial than the actions of those who freed Price. The complicity of the United States government in the institution of slavery stood under judgment.

On May 24, 1859, a large rally to support the imprisoned rescuers was held in Cleveland. Accounts record that several thousand attended the gathering, which was part celebration of abolitionist courage and part protest against federal law. Speaker after speaker denounced the unjust prosecution of those who stood for freedom. Then, near the very end of the program, Asa Mahan, by 1859 president of Adrian College in Michigan, stepped to the stand. He "rejoiced to know that some of the prisoners, whom he had instructed in years past and taught them principles of liberty, were still true to their duty. He felt that he had not lived in vain." Then he added an enigmatic reference to Revelation 19:6: "When the news goes to Michigan, of what you have done here to-day, a voice will go up like the sound of many waters, that 'the Lord God Omnipotent reigneth.'"[2]

---

2   Shipherd, 256.

It was a curious quote from Scripture. Standing among protesters, while those who did right languish in jail, hardly seems like a time to celebrate the reign of God. Yet, this is precisely what President Mahan did. Why? Some might write it off as wishful thinking or as a deeper statement of prophetic insight—the day is coming when right will rule over the land. This second appraisal is not incorrect. Mahan did indeed believe that history was on the side of freedom. Yet his reference to Revelation was, like the rest of his biblical vocabulary, a way to combine both theological and philosophical principle—in this case a way to mix them both with political principle.

Asa Mahan believed that just government upheld the moral law. Unjust government violated the moral law and even made its violation an oppressive demand. One of his earliest efforts to articulate a political philosophy came in 1840, when he released a skeletal integration of metaphysical and ethical teachings: *Abstract of a Course of Lectures on Mental and Moral Philosophy*. Here his discussion of government follows a treatment of moral philosophy. The very idea of law includes two elements: precept and sanction. The former articulates obligation. The later enforces obligation.[3] Citizens are charged with distinguishing between proper and ill-conceived government. Therefore, understanding the appropriate grounds for legitimate government is critical.

Mahan's later, more complete, treatment of these issues is found in his 1848 *Science of Moral Philosophy*. Here he concludes that some commonly claimed grounds for government are incomplete, at best. First, he was skeptical of assertions that true government rests upon the "mere will of God," without consideration of what that will entails. Yet, he also challenged more secular articulations of a "social compact." Mahan believed that just government is grounded in divine authority, but a divine authority that reveals intrinsically right relationships among citizens.[4] Perhaps above all, Mahan believed that government is a means to an end—the

---

3   Asa Mahan, *Abstract of a Course of Lectures on Mental and Moral Philosophy* (Oberlin, Ohio: James Steele, 1840), 229.

4   Asa Mahan, *Science of Moral Philosophy* (Oberlin, Ohio: James M. Fitch, 1848), 201–5.

welfare of each and every member of society. True government is not an arbitrarily divine institution, but it is also no majoritarian compromise among human power brokers. True government serves the people—all of the people, because that is God's intention for creation.

Whenever public discourse finds itself intersecting with this appropriate understanding of government, acknowledgement of God's rule will follow. That rule might not be expressed perfectly—at least not yet—but it exists, nonetheless. Mahan's detailed analysis in his *Moral Philosophy* put it this way: "It is the perception of this great truth on the part of all beings morally pure, which occasions the universal acclaim, 'Alleluia, for the Lord God omnipotent reigneth.' "[5] The college president was willing to get ahead of himself when he saw and touched a truth whose time was coming.

This combination of God's authority and the equality of persons framed Mahan's view. His personal notebook contains reflection on the "law of God." Here he contemplated, "How far shall a precept be extended or what limits shall we assign to it?" His answer: "Nothing can limit the application of a given precept but the same authority by which it was originally given." In short, God's law could not be limited by any other being.[6] At the same time, Mahan's published writing emphasized that this divine law was the protector of human dignity. A government that did not mirror divine intent surrendered its legitimacy.

While Mahan often used the eccentric language of "rulers" and "subjects" when discussing government, he did not do so to support antiquated colonial control. Subjects were not the servants of those with power. They were, in a manner reflecting philosophical language, agents, free beings, those who possessed self-determination. Subjects exercised liberty and individual discernment—subjectivity. A government that ceased to exist for these citizen subjects ceased to be a real government. It became a

---

5   Mahan, 207.

6   Asa Mahan, "Manuscript Writings, Miscellaneous," Archives, Shipman Library, Adrian College, Page 5.

"tyranny," where "subjects cease to be subjects. They become things."[7] It is no surprise that Mahan defined slavery as "the perfection of tyranny."[8] It represented the ultimate decay of relationships, where there were only owners and things. This is what happens when government is no longer a means to the end of human dignity. A government that is an end in itself will inevitably treat someone as a means to the desires of those with power, and this negates the purpose of government, according to the moral law. Others might seek absolute power in order to create some supposed good, but Mahan recognized the danger in such thinking. True to form, he insisted: "I would not change persons to things to save the universe."[9] After all, a universe that tolerated such misuse of power would hardly resemble the universe God intended.

The Oberlin-Wellington rescue case was not resolved as neatly as President Mahan's moral philosophy might require. Instead, a set of counter charges was brought against the kidnappers by antislavery forces, and both sides of the judicial conflict released their prisoners. But this political maneuvering did not dampen Asa Mahan's ardor. After all, for him, the right was the way things ought to be and would someday be—not necessarily the way things were.

The Moral Law in American Imagination

The tension between "ought" and "is" predates the American experiment, but it has been lived throughout the United States with such singularity that we still confront its ironies on a daily basis. Martin Luther King Jr. stood before the Lincoln Memorial in 1963 to talk about a dream, but first he invoked the great discord, even shame, of a nation created from both egalitarian aspirations and the machinery of inequality. To "live out the

---

7   Asa Mahan, *Abstract of a Course of Lectures on Mental and Moral Philosophy*, 234.

8   Mahan, 234.

9   Mahan, 235.

true meaning of its creed" meant to make the transcendent standard a more readily apparent practice.[10]

Political scientists have probed the animating ideas of America's founders. John Locke's philosophy of government, French literati, and thinkers of the Scottish Enlightenment (among others) all contributed to late eighteenth-century notions of nationhood. However, America was always exceptional—and not simply because it saw itself as somehow above the civilizations that came before. In America there was an outlandish political willingness to name aims that far exceeded practice.

Decades have exposed both the genius and hypocrisy of a people who could say that all are created equal and yet live as if some people may be treated as things. The ideal is not to blame for this hypocrisy. Nor does it serve to exonerate injustice. The ideal serves as a standard, debated and redefined. For this reason, the postrevolutionary period was as important as the revolutionary struggle itself. Much of the debate in America over aspirations came after 1776 and even after the ratification of the United States Constitution. A good deal of the debate regarding the American ideal came shortly after the turn of the nineteenth century, and scholars of American intellectual history have suggested that the end of the War of 1812 served as a crucial moment for national conviction.

This is a bit ironic in that the particular war discussed was not necessarily waged for idealistic reasons. Yet, by the year 1815 something had ripened in the American imagination (if not in practice). Writing at the middle of the twentieth century, Yale historian Ralph Henry Gabriel put it this way:

> Americans by 1815 had formulated three major beliefs, each a complex of ideas.
>
> The first tenet assumed the dignity of human personality and asserted the conviction that that dignity could be realized only when the individual was free to express himself and to

---

10 James Melvin Washington, ed., *A Testament of Hope: The Essential Writings of Martin Luther King, Jr.* (San Francisco: Harper & Row, 1986), 219.

participate in decisions of vital import to him. The second tenet assumed that principles of universal validity underlie the common life of men in society, the application of which to affairs makes possible the realization of freedom and dignity. The third tenet asserted that the nation created in 1776 exists as a corporate entity not only to further the peace and security of its citizens but to aid—at home and, by example, abroad—the cause of freedom and humane living.[11]

Human dignity, universal principles, and the ability to share these insights abroad have all come under withering scrutiny in recent decades—and for good reason. Yet beyond the sadness of aims not reached and a long train of abuse, there remains something compelling about these aspirations. If one parses Gabriel's claim, it may be that our failure to live by the third tenet has contributed substantially to a dismissal of the second (universal principles) and a serious questioning of the first (human dignity). These dynamics might be associated with a "postmodern" age, but they are really the product of the great gulf between claim and practice. This kind of cynicism can thrive during any era.

So how did the nascent American republic come to cultivate something like the three tenets identified by Ralph Henry Gabriel? There are many ways to answer this question, but one approach is to begin with the reverence early Americans held for English traditions of law. Not all Americans of the revolutionary and postrevolutionary period came from Anglo cultures, but the separation from Great Britain was not so much a repudiation of English jurisprudence as a desire to be rid of its poor administration.

The esteem many Americans accorded English jurists, such as William Blackstone, serves as one example. Sir William Blackstone (1723–1780) is best remembered for his work in systematizing and then popularizing English legal doctrines. Blackstone began a series of legendary lectures

---

11 Ralph Henry Gabriel, *The Course of American Democratic Thought*, 2nd ed. (New York: The Ronald Press Company, 1956), vi–vii.

on common law in 1753, and this work developed into his four-volume *Commentaries on the Laws of England* (1765–1769). History remembers Blackstone as an eloquent, if not profound, expositor. His analysis was generally appreciated in his native land but practically revered in America. Anecdotes regarding Blackstone's influence throughout early American jurisprudence are legion.

For example, Carl Sandburg's classic (if sentimentalized) study of Abraham Lincoln relates the future president's introduction to Blackstone:

> A mover came by, heading west in a covered wagon. He sold Lincoln a barrel. Lincoln afterward explained, "I did not want it, but to oblige him I bought it, and paid him half a dollar for it." Later, emptying rubbish out of the barrel, he found books at the bottom, Blackstone's *Commentaries on the Laws of England*.
>
> By accident, by a streak of luck, he was owner of the one famous book that young men studying law had to read first of all; it had sneaked into his hands without his expecting it; he remembered his Springfield lawyer-friend, John T. Stuart, saying the law student should read Blackstone first. . . .
>
> So he read Blackstone, the book of lectures delivered by Sir William Blackstone at Oxford, England in 1753. Laws derive their validity from their conformity to the so-called law of nature or law of God. The objects of law are rights and wrongs.[12]

Stories of this sort take on mythic qualities, but it is a fact that many Americans quoted Blackstone outright to defend particular conceptions of right and wrong.

Abolitionist William Hosmer, a Methodist newspaper editor and activist, imported excerpts from Blackstone to bolster his argument for a "higher law" in opposition to the Fugitive Slave legislation. Humanity may endorse statutes contrary to nature and to God, but these are counterfeit laws. Hosmer was especially concerned to cite Blackstone

---

12 Carl Sandburg, *Abraham Lincoln: The Prairie Years*, Vol. 1 (New York: Harcourt, Brace & Company, 1926), 163–64.

on this point: "The law of nature, being coeval with mankind, and dictated by God himself, is of course superior in obligation to any other. It is binding over all the globe, in all countries, and at all times; no human laws are of any validity, if contrary to this; and such of them as are valid derive all their force, and all their authority mediately or immediately, from this original."[13] The studied imprecision of Blackstone's language served American interpreters well. The highest law was considered a law of nature. It was also associated with human nature, and it was said to be dictated by God. Some might claim that this natural law exists apart from any deity. Yet that would not be consistent with Blackstone. Others might argue that this law is identical with Scripture. However, this too, would distort Blackstone's worldview.

The supreme law, as understood by Blackstone, was both a natural law and one dictated by God. The overriding impact of his thought drew a distinction between this transcendent standard and human laws, and he did not shy away from claims of universality. The highest law was something for all times and all places.

Blackstone's articulation of basic relationships between various laws may seem naïve from a contemporary perspective, but it received widespread endorsement during its age. It has also managed to survive in more sophisticated forms. The real stumbling point with Blackstone's formulation did not rest in whether his natural law is or is not dependent upon revelation. The problem came with discerning any detailed definition of this law, its essential quality among human affairs. If there is some law built into human nature, what are its norms? How do we know it when we are faced with living such law? Can we really live its commands?

Questions of this sort force a more diffuse collection of anthropological and theological considerations. Religious traditions have embraced core principles and even some description of a moral law throughout their

---

13 Quoted in William Hosmer, *The Higher Law, in its Relations to Civil Government: With Particular Reference to Slavery, and the Fugitive Slave Law* (Auburn, New York: Derby & Miller, 1852), 48. See William Blackstone, *Commentaries on the Laws of England, Book the First* (Oxford: The Clarendon Press, 1765), 41.

histories. For example, in Judaism, the law is both a sign of relationship with God and with others. Christians have inherited this reverence for the law of God, often considered the moral law. Yet Christians have also differed over the ability to live its claims. Theological conceptions of grace have been accompanied by a bewildering assortment of approaches to the moral law. The Reformation controversies regarding law and grace did not create Enlightenment moral reflection, but seventeenth- and eighteenth-century thinking carried echoes of earlier conversation. The ambivalent relationship that Protestant traditions lived with the concept of God's law is particularly illuminating.

The Protestant Ethic and the Definition of Moral Law

One might assume that there was in Western Christian thought a simple dichotomy between those who believed we could live God's law by human effort and those who agonized over sin and failure to measure up. That, at least, is the popular narrative of the sixteenth century. Traditions now known as "Catholic" have always held special reverence for the natural law. This expression of faith also designed an elaborate sacramental system to serve as a meeting ground between law and grace. Protestant conflicts with church authority and insight regarding the unearned brilliance of grace sometimes led to a repudiation of "the law." Early Protestant commentators might suggest that the law was real and even critical to spiritual self-understanding—but only as a reminder of our imperfection. There were later expressions of Protestantism that attempted to retrieve a more positive perspective, one that appreciated the law as a blueprint for righteous living, but this blueprint did not offer a means toward salvation so much as a way to discern if one's actions were properly led by the Spirit.

Linking understandings of the law with human destiny was crucial. If our effort cannot guarantee a following of the law, how are we saved? If we are saved by grace alone, then how do we know the state and destiny of our soul? Is there any way to trust whether we have received grace? These questions may strike contemporary folk as a head game, but they were (and still are) real.

The inclination of Protestant thinkers to emphasize the law as a reminder of sin or as merely a restraint for extreme behavior was not universal. John Calvin (1509–1564), for one, gave voice to a "third" use of the law that suggested a more positive function. The law could not save, but it could clarify and teach God's ways. Still, this willingness to see the law as a guide might be conceptualized in very severe terms. According to Calvin: "The law is to the flesh like a whip to an idle and balky ass, to arouse it to work."[14] It is no accident that Calvin invoked the language of labor. A strange paradox developed among many forms of Protestantism. While the sin of "works righteousness" was condemned, most Protestant traditions came to expect that the faithful would work and work diligently.

This expectation arose for many reasons, but it was perhaps strongest among later followers of Calvin, who struggled under the doctrine of predestination. The absolute dependence upon God's fiat for salvation made it difficult to know whether one stood among the elect. This spiritual anxiety was navigated by both embracing the law and denying that it could be an instrument for salvation. Instead, the law became a measure of the general good created by one's life, and this good, in turn, indicated whether one possessed God's favor.

The classic and controversial exploration of these dynamics, of course, appeared in Max Weber's thesis *The Protestant Ethic and the Spirit of Capitalism* (1905). Our purpose here is not to repeat every point of Weber or to rehearse more than one hundred years of critical response. Rather, we simply note Weber's overall thesis as it relates to evolving conceptions of the moral law. When Weber addressed the Calvinist vision of creation, he had this to say: "The wonderfully purposeful organization and arrangement of this cosmos is, according both to the revelation of the Bible and to natural intuition, evidently designed by God to serve the utility of the human race. This makes labour in the service of impersonal

---

14 John Calvin, *Institutes of the Christian Religion*, Vol. 1, ed. John T. McNeill, trans. Ford Lewis Battles (Philadelphia: The Westminster Press, 1960), 361.

social usefulness appear to promote the glory of God and hence to be willed by Him."[15] Such a rationale for hard work was not intended as theological sleight of hand. Serving the glory of God remained everything among this tradition. Yet the tendency to examine outcomes for signs of salvation did make many forms of Protestantism susceptible to consequentialist ethics—systems where results determined judgments regarding right and wrong.

According to Weber, a mix of theological doctrine, anxiety, and worldly measurement fueled the capitalist economies of the seventeenth century. Debate regarding the accuracy of this thesis is ongoing, but one cannot deny a turn toward analysis of outcomes. The worldly asceticism identified by Weber kept a diligent eye on results, but work was celebrated as a sacred task for the benefit of God and others. Such a systematized attitude toward labor often led to surplus accumulation of resources, and this did raise a thorny question: Was the amassing of wealth good or evil?

If wealth had a generally negative reputation among purer forms of commonplace Catholicism, it was a potential sign of God's favor for many Protestants. This did not mean that wealth was to be squandered through self-indulgence. It was, for rich and poor alike, to serve the glory of God. Again, Weber: "Wealth is thus bad ethically only in so far as it is a temptation to idleness and sinful enjoyment of life, and its acquisition is bad only when it is with the purpose of later living merrily and without care. But as a performance of duty in a calling it is not only morally permissible, but actually enjoined."[16] To some extent, wealth might even be interpreted as a sign of grace and poverty a sign of divine rebuke.

As with all re-configurations of the moral law, the Calvinist version suggested a shift in the understanding of means and ends. While commenting on Weber's thesis, R. H. Tawney captured the inversion characteristic of the movement: "Labour is not merely an economic means: it is

---

15 Max Weber, *The Protestant Ethic and the Spirit of Capitalism*, trans. Talcott Parsons (New York: Charles Scribner's Sons, 1958), 109.

16 Weber, 163.

a spiritual end."[17] Such an elevation of work promised much. It bore the potential of respecting within every person a profound calling, and this would appear to be the tradition's sober intent. Yet in practice this shift from instrumental value to objective aim left a mixed moral legacy. A people who work to eat and care for necessities can do so apart from identifying who they are with what they do or how well they perform. Such is not possible for a people who have made labor a spiritual end in itself. This viewpoint can facilitate a valuing of the self and others precisely according to the quality of labor or the quantity of production.

In short, it is easier to treat people as means to an end among a complicated theological culture that sanctifies the results of labor. Some might read the thesis of Weber as demonstrating a self-interest that arises from Protestant spiritual insecurity. One need not accept this judgment to appreciate the way issues of means and ends were altered during the sixteenth and seventeenth centuries. Even the most altruistic believers can wind up endorsing the manipulation of others for an end that appears so splendid.

Weber argued that there was a trajectory to the whole Protestant ethic. Near the close of his thesis, he quoted John Wesley (1703–1791) at length to suggest that the eighteenth century saw the connection between work and spiritual dignity disintegrate. Wesley may not have toiled under the anxiety-producing doctrine of predestination, but he did help create a movement of disciplined people who sought to integrate the spiritual and the practical. Weber noted that Wesley, an observer in real time, struggled with the inevitable problems of such rigor. Various redactions of the Wesley passage have appeared in print. The quote below is from Thomas Jackson's 1872 edition of *The Works of John Wesley*:

> It nearly concerns us to understand how the case stands with us at present. I fear, wherever riches have increased, (exceeding few are the exceptions,) the essence of religion, the mind that was in Christ, has decreased in the same proportion. Therefore do I not see how it is possible, in the nature of things, for any revival of

---

17 Weber, 3.

true religion to continue long. For religion must necessarily produce both industry and frugality; and these cannot but produce riches. But as riches increase, so will pride, anger, and love of the world in all its branches.[18]

Wesley's antidote was to rely on the threefold pattern made iconic in his sermon "The Use of Money." The legendary triad of gaining, saving, and giving follows inherited counsel, with the exception that Wesley made his third and final command the absolutely necessary conclusion of such living. The only hope for a vital faith among rigorous people is generosity—a giving away—as powerful as any industry.[19]

Wesley's legacy regarding labor and means and ends has been evaluated in myriad ways. His movement's internalizing of generally Protestant practices places him near the end of an arc which considered work an expression of faithfulness. But his unwillingness to consider accumulation a sign of capricious favor set him apart. Wesley understood that economic strength can come from certain worldly behaviors, but this privilege could not be rationalized as a sign of spiritual blessing. This may leave the contemporary observer uncomfortable and underwhelmed. John Wesley did not usher in a completely organic or structural analysis of economic forces. His recourse to generosity may strike some as feeble, unsophisticated, and limited in its effect to create equity. Yet one must remember that Wesley's primary concern was the creation of a faithful people, and the fact that he saw economic power as a threat to authentic faith should not be overlooked. Giving did not solve the cultural assumptions that drove inequality, but it did provide a limit for measuring divine favor according to worldly success.

---

18 John Wesley, "Thoughts Upon Methodism," in *The Works of John Wesley*, ed., Thomas Jackson, Vol. 13, *Letters* (Grand Rapids, Michigan: Baker Book House, 1986), 260. See the treatment of this text in Weber, *The Protestant Ethic and the Spirit of Capitalism*, 175–76.

19 John Wesley, *The Works of John Wesley*, ed. Albert C. Outler, Vol. 2, in *Sermons II*, 34–70 (Nashville: Abingdon Press, 1985), 263–80.

Reason and Results

Among English-speaking religious movements, John Wesley's is hard to define. He represented the close of an era but also the almost explosive beginning of a revival. He respected the emphasis upon reason in religious reflection, but his ministry was nothing without an appreciation for the heart. By the end of the eighteenth century, more purely philosophical currents clarified two distinct approaches to the moral law.

The first approach would evolve from a variety of thinkers and stress the intrinsic quality of action. Behaviors were either right or wrong in themselves. The second approach would evolve from a concern to quantify outcomes. Behaviors were either right or wrong to the extent that they created some good result. The first, of course, has come down to us as the deontological school of thought. The second has been inherited as the teleological or consequentialist view.

For centuries scholars and teachers have debated whether the moral law could be defined by one of these two approaches, but we often forget that this was a conversation with great subtlety and variation. Moreover, the codification and formal naming of these overarching approaches is typically credited to C. D. Broad's 1930 text, *Five Types of Ethical Theory*.[20] Not too many decades following Broad's twentieth-century work, ethicists began dismissing the general tension between deontology and teleology in search of a third way. This does not mean that Broad was wrong, but it does point out that longstanding movements often receive explicit analysis and definition close to the end of their dominance, at the precise time they are falling out of fashion.

The fact that these two competing visions received so much formal reflection near the end of their popularity almost guaranteed problems in interpretation. The variegated history of contrast was collapsed into over-simplification and then discarded. However, categorization and dismissal are not a route toward better understanding. The sharp edges of earlier

---

20 C. D. Broad, *Five Types of Ethical Theory* (London: Routledge and Kegan Paul, 1930).

conversation should not be smoothed over by contemporary opinions, and the multitude of differentiations should not be forgotten. There were, to be sure, two distinct approaches to the moral law, but the story is much more fluid than our contemporary scholarship often admits. The story is also more interesting and revealing. Ultimately, it is a story that has much to teach us today.

While deontology and its assumptions regarding inherent values may be viewed as a "default" position in ethics, the eighteenth century witnessed the rise of self-identified teleological (consequentialist) systems. There were (and still are) a bewildering variety of teleological approaches to ethics. The kind that developed in England during the eighteenth century took the concern for "utility" and transformed it into an organized "utilitarianism." We often think of utilitarianism as an early or mid-nineteenth-century English phenomenon—one with relatively secular commitments—but it really had its roots in a religiously inspired form of eighteenth-century thinking.

Among this movement, William Paley (1743–1805) served as the dean of "theological utilitarianism."[21] Paley was born in Peterborough, Northamptonshire, and educated at Christ College, Cambridge. He developed as a fellow and tutor at Cambridge and was ordained in 1767. His lectures at the university were well received and served as the foundation for much of his later publication. Paley became a younger friend of Edmund Law, bishop of Carlisle and was indebted to Law in many ways. Today many think of William Paley as the Archdeacon of Carlisle, and his principal work on ethics (1785) is dedicated to Bishop Edmund Law.

While William Paley is remembered as the authoritative exponent of theological utilitarianism, his ideas were not particularly original. A small

---

21 One of the most concise treatments of this movement is: Graham Cole, "Theological Utilitarianism and the Eclipse of the Theistic Sanction," *Tyndale Bulletin* 42, no. 2 (November 1991): 226–44. Now-classic examinations are: Wilson Smith, "William Paley's Theological Utilitarianism in America," *The William and Mary Quarterly* 11, no. 3 (July 1954): 402–24, and Wendell Glick, "Bishop Paley in America," *The New England Quarterly* 27, no. 3 (September 1954): 347–54.

but dedicated group of forebears, most from Cambridge, prepared the ground for this movement. Perhaps most significant as an early text was John Gay's *Dissertation Concerning the Fundamental Principle of Virtue or Morality* (1731). Gay (1699–1745), not surprisingly, rooted his system of ethics in an interpretation of God's will. Yet Gay inevitably encountered the problem of defining that will. He ended up arguing that God's goodness and presumed happiness meant that the divine will intended the happiness of humanity. Thus Gay stood within that tradition that stressed the goal of happiness as a primary good.[22]

This connection between happiness and "the good" is not insignificant. There were thinkers in ethics who contrasted a concern for "the good" with a concern for "the right." The former often developed teleological or consequentialist theories. The latter often developed deontological emphases. These two values were not necessarily in conflict, but they could find themselves at loggerheads. What happens when the identified good requires doing something contrary to the right? What happens when the identified right prevents one from creating a good or even the greatest good? Such questions, reconfigured and reconceptualized over many generations, animated much debate in ethics.

William Paley's primary, almost definitive, contribution to this conversation came with the publication of *The Principles of Moral and Political Philosophy* in 1785. By 1786 the book had gone through three editions and was a part of the curriculum at Cambridge.[23] Paley spoke from a different place than earlier representatives of the Calvinist tradition. His urbane and flexible Anglicanism did not follow the pattern of more severe Protestantism. When reading Paley, one is not confronted with detailed qualifications that stress the moral law's inability to create salvation. Yet he shared a deep concern for evaluating matters of right and wrong according to results, even though the doctrinal logic differed.

---

22 Graham Cole, "Theological Utilitarianism and the Eclipse of the Theistic Sanction," 229–31.

23 Cole, 240.

Paley, as might be expected, made an analysis of happiness seminal to his moral philosophy. Here he defined happiness as a condition "in which the amount or aggregate of pleasure exceeds that of pain; and the degree of happiness depends upon the quantity of this excess."[24] Paley did not understand happiness entirely in terms of worldly pleasure, as some might suggest. He devoted eighteen pages to his exploration of the matter and employed more nuance than is typically acknowledged.[25]

Still, happiness, as a concept, shaped much of Paley's ethic when it came to defining virtue. Perhaps the most quoted piece from Paley's entire text is the one that reads: "Virtue is, the doing good to mankind, in obedience to the will of God, and for the sake of everlasting happiness."[26] This definition placed Paley squarely within the tradition of consequentialist ethics, which is no surprise, but its constituent parts invite further reflection. The doing of good was a common enough obligation. Yet Paley made this mundane commitment a theological issue by placing it under the will of God. A pattern of logic akin to others can be found here, but the attention given "everlasting happiness" raised additional questions. In one sense, the appreciation for happiness simply expressed something that was to be shared with others. Everlasting happiness could be understood as part and parcel of the good extended toward humanity.

In another sense, Paley argued that the happiness named was at stake for those exercising moral commitments. People who did God's will by advancing the good would enjoy eternal life—everlasting happiness. Those who did not, risked their heavenly destiny. At one point Paley put it this way, "Therefore, private happiness is our motive, and the will of God our rule."[27] He followed by saying: "in acts of duty as well as acts of prudence, we consider solely what we shall gain or lose by the act."[28] This

---

24 William Paley, *The Principles of Moral and Political Philosophy*, 3rd ed. (London: R. Faulder, 1786), 18.
25 Paley, 18–35.
26 Paley, 36.
27 Paley, 52.
28 Paley, 53.

expression of the ethic led critics to charge that Paley made proper behavior a matter of self-interest, and even without self-interest as the overriding motivation, there were questions regarding the essentially utilitarian criteria for Paley's version of the moral law.

When closing his treatise, Paley applied the ethic of theological utilitarianism to understandings of civil law and government. In a section titled "The Duty of Submission to Civil Government Explained" the term "expediency" is employed to capture all commitments of citizenship. Paley stated: "We assign for the only ground of the subject's obligation, the will of God as collected from expediency."[29] By expediency, Paley implied a cost-benefit analysis of the consequences that follow either obeying or resisting civil law: in short, a utilitarian calculous of potential outcomes.[30]

As an application of his ethic to civil discourse and behavior, this formula might be expected, but many were troubled by the detached rationale. For instance, Paley is remembered for his mildly antislavery commitments. He was a gradualist, which may not command much respect today. Yet he was, at least, on the right side of the issue. However, his calculating theories regarding government and civic participation tended to reinforce the status quo. Paley meant something more principled than many imagine when he used the term "expediency," but in retrospect, the whole pattern of reasoning came up short.

During the later 1840s Henry David Thoreau famously confronted William Paley in his essay now known as "Civil Disobedience." According to Thoreau: "Paley appears never to have contemplated those cases to which the rule of expediency does not apply, in which a people, as well as an individual, must do justice, cost what it may."[31] Such criticism was not

---

29 Paley, 423.

30 William M. Wiecek, "Latimer: Lawyers, Abolitionists, and the Problem of Unjust Laws," in *Antislavery Reconsidered: New Perspectives on the Abolitionists*, eds. Lewis Perry and Michael Fellman (Baton Rouge: Louisiana State University Press, 1979), 224.

31 Henry David Thoreau, *Walden and Civil Disobedience: Authoritative Texts, Background Reviews, and Essays in Criticism*, ed. Owen Thomas (New York: W. W. Norton & Company, 1966), 227.

limited to the greater Boston area. A variety of thinkers from a variety of places raised similar objections to Paley's ethic between the years 1785 and 1861, the beginning of the American Civil War.

The Moral Sense and the Moral Law

The story of European moral philosophy in the eighteenth century is full of both basic patterns and surprising turns. As with many disciplines, students have noted characteristic differences between Continental thinking and that rooted in Great Britain. For instance, English-speaking thinkers were especially keen on empirical foundations for their theories. Continental schools (from several different languages and cultures) often sought universal truths beyond experience. However, these generalities should not be overstated, and when it came to the distinction between deontological and teleological moral views, the assumptions break down almost completely.

One example is the contrast between the theological utilitarianism of William Paley (and those of his movement) and English-speaking commentators of a decidedly deontological stamp. The conflict in this case often revolved around differing views regarding the "moral sense" or the "conscience." Paley had this to say about claims regarding some moral sense or conscience:

> Upon the whole, it seems to me, either that there exist no such instincts as compose what is called the moral sense, or that they are not now to be distinguished from prejudices and habits; on which account they cannot be depended upon in moral reasoning; I mean that it is not a safe way of arguing, to assume certain principles as so many dictates, impulses, and instincts of nature, and then to draw conclusions from these principles, as to the rectitude or wrongness of actions, independent of the tendency of such actions, or of any other consideration whatever.[32]

---

32 William Paley, *The Principles of Moral and Political Philosophy*, 16.

As Paley saw things, determining right and wrong through a "moral sense" was too arbitrary. Only the "tendency" of actions to produce desired results could be relied on with any consistency.

This dismissal of the moral sense ran contrary to a tradition that had been developing in Scotland for several decades. Identifying the exact beginning of this movement is difficult, but perhaps Francis Hutcheson (1694–1746) deserves special mention.[33] The Scottish emphasis upon a moral sense received encyclopedic endorsement from later writers, especially Thomas Reid (1710–1796), James Beattie (1735–1803), and Dugald Stewart (1753–1828). Our primary concern is for this school's approach to moral theory, but one must acknowledge that Scottish defense of a moral sense followed certain commitments in metaphysics and epistemology.

Thomas Reid (and followers) came to be known as Common Sense Realists. This terminology described the way these thinkers trusted a common human ability to know things with a general degree of accuracy. In an age when more skeptical philosophers wondered if experience could be relied on to reveal truths, Reid trusted his perceptions. Unlike John Locke, he did not place an intermediate world of ideas between experience and knowledge. For Reid and his students, experience gave a direct, immediate awareness of the world outside. In 1764 he published his *Inquiry into the Human Mind, on the Principles of Common Sense*.

Reid became affiliated with the University of Glasgow and further refined his work in epistemology. *Essays on the Intellectual Powers of Man* appeared in 1785, and the application of this philosophy to ethics was published in 1788, when Reid released his *Essays on the Active Powers of Man*. It is within this latter work that Reid emphasized the moral sense or the conscience as a trustworthy guide. He likened this ethical power to other faculties, but he also clarified his conception of its role in moral judgment:

---

33 D. H. Meyer, *The Instructed Conscience: The Shaping of the American National Ethic* (Philadelphia: University of Pennsylvania Press, 1972), 36.

It is of small consequence what name we give to this moral power of the human mind; but it is so important a part of our constitution, as to deserve an appropriated name. The name of *conscience*, as it is the most common, seems to me as proper as any that has been given it. I find no fault with the name *moral sense*, although I conceive this name has given occasion to some mistakes concerning the nature of our moral power. Modern Philosophers have conceived of the external senses as having no other office but to give us certain sensations, or simple conceptions, which we could not have without them. And this notion has been applied to the moral sense. But it seems to me a mistaken notion in both. By the sense of seeing, I not only have the conception of the different colours, but I perceive one body to be of this colour, another of that. In like manner, by my moral sense, I not only have the conceptions of right and wrong in conduct, but I perceive *this* conduct to be right, *that* to be wrong, and *that* indifferent.[34]

Reid's distinctions are very important. He sought a firm foundation that did not rely on utility for determining right and wrong, but critics suspected that moral sense theorists overstated their case. Could we really have such an immediate, accurate discernment of things in ethics?

Reid and his followers attempted to emphasize that this conscience or moral sense did not simply make capricious judgments. It was grounded in the moral law. With a nod to Jeremiah 31:33, Reid wrote: "That conscience, which is in every man's breast, is the law of God written in his heart, which he cannot disobey without acting unnaturally, and being self-condemned."[35] This meticulously articulated philosophy was open to attack by skeptics, but it also provided a certain degree of intellectual credibility to something other than utilitarianism. Because morality was a matter of perceiving right and wrong intuitively, it avoided consequentialist

---

34 Thomas Reid, *Essays on the Active Powers of Man* (Edinburgh: John Bell, Parliament-Square; London: G. G. J. & J. Robinson, 1788), 407–8.

35 Reid, 374.

calculations. Human behavior was judged according to values that were considered inherent.

Reid's school elevated the reputation of deontological approaches and provided an option for many in the church who could not embrace William Paley. In fact, it is difficult to discuss antebellum ethics in America without encountering the presumption that Scottish Common Sense was the only viable option for moral theorists. As we will see, American moral reflection before the Civil War was more diverse than this assumption, but a considerable number of writers and teachers and public servants were indebted to Thomas Reid (and especially Dugald Stewart) for their ideas.

One of the ironies among this tradition can be found in the way Reid labored to categorize ideas. He was a tireless observer of the mind and its operations, and yet he is remembered as someone who brought epistemology and ethics down to earth. He was at once the learned doctor and the teacher who sought to emphasize abilities we all hold in common. Not everything about Reid and his legacy led to democratic conviction, but some in America endorsed his philosophy precisely because it spoke to qualities considered part of being human. In an oblique way, Reid's ethic forced fans and detractors alike to explore what it means to be a person. Philosophers had done this before, and many would do so later. However, the notion that each and every person possesses certain faculties or powers made the conversation inevitable at a time when civic participation and political recognition were at stake.

We could write off Thomas Reid and those of this school as impractical dreamers or dull theoreticians. After all, they did not provide the cleanest formula for determining right from wrong, and they certainly did not aim their moral philosophy toward getting results. Yet it would be a mistake to dismiss them. Their claims to certainty of perception might be stretched beyond contemporary comfort, but there was a certain intellectual integrity about them. For many years now, religious traditions that were once animated by Scottish Common Sense have sought to distance themselves from this history. The emphasis on common abilities, moral intuition, and things being what they appear to be fell out of favor a long time ago. It is almost a rite of cultural advancement to stereotype the legacy left by Reid and his students—before repudiating it altogether.[36]

Still, something about this witness in both epistemology and morals reached further and deeper than often thought. For instance, contemporary observer Maurice Lee has argued that Scottish Common Sense influenced the intellectual development of Frederick Douglass (1818–1895) and even contributed to what some call his second emancipation.[37] After leaving slavery, Douglass was embraced by antislavery activists in New England, but he confronted the manipulative way some in this movement attempted to use him for their aims. Douglass, convinced of his own faculties and gifts, challenged such behavior.[38] His second autobiography, *My Bondage and My Freedom* (1855) displayed subtle appreciation for "common sense." Lee contends that Douglass was inspired by his friend James McCune Smith (1813–1865), a Scottish-educated physician of African descent. Smith wrote the preface to this second autobiography.

By demanding recognition of his own intellectual and moral powers, Douglass refused to simply narrate his victimization. Instead, he analyzed slavery's injustice through the lens of experience and insisted upon defining the *meaning* of this experience for himself. His second birth was demonstrated geographically when Douglass moved from New England to the western regions of New York State.

The far-reaching impact of Reid's school can be demonstrated even more with reference to the life of Elizabeth Margaret Chandler (1807–1834). Born a Quaker near Wilmington, Delaware, Chandler lost her mother and father at an early age. She lived among extended family in Philadelphia and then moved with some of them to the wilderness of

---

36 This more recent dynamic is explored in Christopher P. Momany, "Faculty Psychology in the Holiness Theology of Asa Mahan," *The Asbury Journal* 69, no. 2 (Fall 2014): 136–47.

37 Maurice S. Lee, *Slavery, Philosophy, and American Literature, 1830–1860* (Cambridge: Cambridge University Press, 2005), 93–132.

38 Frederick Douglass, *My Bondage and My Freedom* in *Frederick Douglass Autobiographies* (New York: The Library of America, 1994), 367.

Michigan. Chandler was a published poet of note, writing to advance the antislavery cause and the role of women in civic leadership. She also expressed a profound appreciation for nature.

Chandler was a voracious reader and kept track of developments in theology and philosophy from her remote home in southeastern Michigan Territory. In one piece of correspondence she remarked that she valued the study of "Mental Philosophy" (metaphysics and epistemology): "It is like being endowed with a new intellect, or gifted suddenly with another sense."[39] She also shared: "I have lately read a little work of Reid's, on the Mind, but which enters into little more than the alphabet of the science."[40] We cannot identify the "little work" mentioned, and it is difficult to imagine that anything Reid wrote might be so characterized. Yet the fact that an especially talented literary advocate for abolition would read Scottish Common Sense out in the Old Northwest during the early 1830s says something. How the mind works and how it determines right and wrong mattered for those committed to equality.

Means and Ends and the Moral Law

Not every representative of Scottish philosophy agreed with Reid and his followers. David Hume (1711–1776) is perhaps the most obvious example. Hume has become legendary as an Enlightenment skeptic. He shared much with his Scottish colleagues, especially the reliance on experience to generate understanding, but where others saw experience as a trustworthy guide, Hume was not so sure. His eloquent essays, insightful wit, and way of backing philosophical claims into a corner won him friend and foe alike. Hume remains a monumental figure in philosophy, and most contemporary treatments grant him extensive time and space. One is much more likely to find readings from David Hume in today's undergraduate anthologies than essays from Thomas Reid, and there are several reasons

---

39 Quoted in Elizabeth Margaret Chandler, *The Poetical Works of Elizabeth Margaret Chandler*, ed. Benjamin Lundy (Philadelphia: Lemuel Howell, 1836), 36.

40 Chandler, 36.

for this phenomenon. The perennially fashionable nature of skepticism may contribute to Hume's longevity.

Many would interpret the later versions of Scottish Common Sense as a response to Hume's skepticism. Yet Hume's challenge to intellectual assumptions reached beyond Scotland. Immanuel Kant's philosophy did not claim that experience could supply an indisputable grip on reality, but his whole project did, in several ways, respond to the problems raised by David Hume. Kant's *Prolegomena to Every Future Metaphysic* (written in 1783 and translated into the English by Scot, John Richardson in 1819) contains a now iconic admission by the German philosopher: "I freely own it was Hume's hint that first roused me from a dogmatic slumber of many years, and gave quite a new direction to my researches in that field of speculative philosophy."[41] Immanuel Kant would be remembered as the personification of transcendental speculation regarding metaphysics and epistemology. However, his moral philosophy was equally important.

Kant (1724–1804) was born in Konigsberg, East Prussia (now a part of the Russian Federation), to a family of modest means. A disciplined Protestant Pietism dominated the Kant home, and over the years many have suggested that this culture shaped the philosopher's method and rigor, if not his actual religious beliefs. We should pause, though, before handing along stereotypes regarding Immanuel Kant. Stories are legion about his scripted adherence to a schedule and his purported provincialism. He died in the city of his birth. Yet Kant was actually no dour professor of unexamined habits. He served as a popular teacher and someone with refined social graces, including a sharp sense of humor.[42] Kant is easy to typecast, perhaps especially because of his dense and almost tortured philosophical reasoning, but he deserves a nuanced appraisal.

---

41 Immanuel Kant, *Prolegomena to Every Future Metaphysic, which Can Appear as a Science*, trans. John Richardson (London: W. Simpkin and R. Marshall, 1819) in *Metaphysical Works of the Celebrated Immanuel Kant*, trans. John Richardson (London, 1836), xi.

42 H. J. Paton, *The Categorical Imperative: A Study in Kant's Moral Philosophy* (Chicago: University of Chicago Press, 1948), 197–98.

Immanuel Kant's overarching contribution might be described as a search for certainty without resort to empirical evidences. He did not deny the world of experience, but he took Hume's reservations seriously. What could experience really confirm about cause and effect, for instance? Kant developed an elaborate system that appreciated experience and the limited, though necessary, role it played in understanding—while reaching for a universal and eternal certainty beyond experience. Once he devoted himself to this task, his seminal work appeared in 1781 as *Critique of Pure Reason*. *Prolegomena* followed in 1783, and the watershed text on ethics was released in 1785 as *Groundwork of the Metaphysic of Morals*.

With the publication of *Groundwork*, Kant introduced his "Categorical Imperative." The principle was refined in later writings, especially *Critique of Practical Reason* (1788) and *The Metaphysics of Morals* (1797), but the 1785 work inaugurated a new approach to what was later termed "deontological ethics." *Groundwork of the Metaphysic of Morals* is not very long, and Kant seemed to intend it as a clear expression of his "Categorical Imperative." Yet with Kant things were rarely simple, and subsequent scholars have squabbled over the various versions of the Imperative. Is there really one, fundamental Imperative? Are there three articulations of the one Imperative? Are there even more variations?

Writing in the middle of the twentieth century, H. J. Paton offered this intriguing comment: "We might have expected Kant to be content with one formulation of the categorical imperative. Instead he embarrasses us with no less than five different formulae, though, curiously enough, he tends to speak as if there were only three."[43] Paton, we should note, was a revered Scottish philosopher following in the footsteps of those who translated and then interpreted Kant for the English-speaking world.[44]

John Richardson may have been the first of this Scottish tradition, and Paton kept it alive during and following World War II. However, the

---

43 Paton, 129.

44 J. H. Burns, "Scottish Kantians: An Exploration," *Journal of Scottish Philosophy* 7, no. 2 (August 2009): 115–31.

Scot who translated Kant at a critical time for America was John William (J. W.) Semple, a graduate of Glasgow (1822). Semple released a lengthy book that combined *Groundwork of the Metaphysic of Morals* with some of Kant's other ethical reflection in 1836. This piece, titled simply *The Metaphysic of Ethics*, was published in Edinburgh and included a one-hundred-page introduction.

Semple's rendering of Kant around how we might number the Categorical Imperative reads as follows:

> The three expressions just adopted, enouncing the principle of morality, are no more than three *"formulae"* of one and the same law, each involving in it the other two; and any difference is subjectively, not objectively, practical. They vary by giving a sensible delineation, according to different analogies, to an idea of reason, approaching it thereby to the mental vision and its feelings. Accordingly all maxims have—
>
> I. A form, consisting in their universality; and here the tenor of the categorical imperative was, "All maxims shall be such only as are fit for law universal."
>
> II. A matter, *i.e.* an end; where the formula ordained, that each Intelligent, being by his nature an end in himself, should subordinate to this end the maxims of all his casual and arbitrary ends.
>
> III. An aggregate determination, by the formula, that all maxims of the self-legislative will must be totally subordinated to, and resolved into, the potential idea of the realm of ends, like as if it were the realm of nature.[45]

In essence, Kant summarized the Categorical Imperative as a framework for (1) universalizing the moral law, (2) applying that law to people as ends in themselves, and then (3) working out the relationships among society where a universalized moral law respects people as ends in themselves.

---

45 Immanuel Kant, *The Metaphysic of Ethics*, trans. J. W. Semple (Edinburgh: Thomas Clark, 1836), 44, 53–54.

H. J. Paton put it this way: "In the final review three formulae only are mentioned: (1) the Formula of the Law of Nature, (2) the Formula of the End in Itself, and (3) the Formula of the Kingdom of Ends. The first formula is said to be concerned with the form of a moral maxim—that is, with its universality; the second with its matter—that is, with its ends; while the third combines both form and matter."[46] Kant retains a deserved reputation for being difficult to grasp, but this treatment of the Imperative conveyed a certain elegance.

Something like this understanding of the Categorical Imperative was probably floating about the mind of President Asa Mahan when he made his remarks to that crowd in Cleveland in 1859. Mahan defined the moral law as a "universal" obligation. He also stressed that people should never be treated as mere means to an end. Mahan's 1848 *Science of Moral Philosophy* includes a lengthy quote from Semple's translation of Kant. The college president stressed that a person

> can not be taken for a bare means, conducive either to his own or to other persons' ends, but must be esteemed an end in himself; that is to say, he is invested with an internal dignity (an absolute worth,) in name of which, he extorts reverence for his person, from every other finite intelligent throughout the universe, and is entitled to compare himself with all such, and to deem himself their equal.[47]

There are also indications that Asa Mahan considered the larger world of social interaction according to Kant's third dynamic—the kingdom or realm of ends. This notion of an order that combines the universal law with the dignity of each person embraced both the self and others. For

---

46 Immanuel Kant, *Groundwork of the Metaphysic of Morals*, trans. H. J. Paton (New York: Harper & Row, Publishers, 1964), 36.

47 Asa Mahan, *Science of Moral Philosophy*, 268. Mahan's quote is taken from Semple's translation of Kant's *The Metaphysic of Ethics*, 274.

instance, at one point Mahan wrote that there are duties people owe to themselves because they inhabit "a realm of ends."[48]

Kant's Categorical Imperative exerted a profound influence on the social and even political thinking of Asa Mahan. His lectures regarding the United States Constitution, written against the backdrop of America's Civil War, are particularly animated by these values. The college president spoke of the relationships embodied through means and ends in good government: "Government, to answer its ends, must be the citadel of liberty to all its subjects & render each & all free & equal in the enjoyment of life, liberty, & the pursuit of happiness."[49] There is a subtle twist of logic here. Mahan understood government to be a means to an end, but this role as a means served the highest of values, namely the dignity of those who are ends in themselves. Moreover, the language of "each & all" mirrors the Categorical Imperative's concern for matter or ends, on the one hand, and form or universality, on the other hand. Asa Mahan presented the Constitution as a blueprint for implementing the Declaration of Independence, and, in the process, he described a national community that sounded very much like Immanuel Kant's "realm of ends."

---

48 Mahan, 269.

49 Asa Mahan, "Manuscript Writings, Miscellaneous," Archives, Shipman Library, Adrian College, 227.

Two

THE GOOD FOR WHOM?

New England Traditions of Teleological Ethics

Years ago, while beginning graduate studies in Princeton, I found time one fall Friday afternoon to walk downtown and visit the local cemetery. The leaves were stunning—oranges and yellows on a clear day of crystal sunlight and intermittent shadows. I knew the great eighteenth-century theologian, Jonathan Edwards, was buried nearby. I read his work in my undergraduate studies at a small Midwestern college. Was I really in the place where his ministry and witness came to a close? The grave offered conclusive testimony. I was somewhat embarrassed for reasons that still escape me, but I felt drawn to the master's resting place. I share this memory only after learning that I am not alone, and such curiosity is not limited to my generation. Recently, one of my undergraduate students visited the same university community, and before I knew it, he was texting photographs of the Edwards grave to me and to others.

Jonathan Edwards (1703–1758) remains a legendary figure in American religious history.[1] Though buried in New Jersey, he is best known for his lifetime of work throughout New England. Edwards was born in East Windsor, Connecticut, and was graduated from Yale College in 1720. He

---

1 One of the more recent approaches to the legacy of Edwards is expressed through a multidisciplinary collection of essays, Oliver D. Crisp and Douglas A. Sweeney, eds., *After Jonathan Edwards: The Courses of the New England Theology* (Oxford: Oxford University Press, 2012).

received the MA from Yale in 1724 and soon began a life-defining ministry with his grandfather, Solomon Stoddard, in Northampton, Massachusetts. Following the death of Stoddard, Edwards assumed leadership of both a theological movement and an ecclesiastical tradition. Today Edwards is remembered as a brilliant figure who preserved and redefined the Calvinist lineage in America. He was also one of the few colonial intellectuals to receive attention far beyond his isolated context. In 1758 the Calvinists at Princeton prevailed upon Edwards to assume the presidency of that institution. Edwards, a defender of traditional beliefs *and* learned supporter of medical developments, received a smallpox inoculation in Princeton. He died of complications from the vaccine soon after taking office.

Many readers of Edwards have a hard time getting past his erudite and sometimes harsh sermons. Those who devote more energy—even a lifetime of study—can find themselves consumed by the treatment Edwards gave to particular doctrines or the way he both embodied and changed his culture. Some have addressed the implications of his theology for ethics. This last concern informs our present study. The views that Edwards advanced on matters of the will certainly relate to this question, but of particular importance is the posthumous essay, *The Nature of True Virtue*, published in 1765.

This short but pithy text explores a distinction between true and natural virtue. Unlike many contemporary commentators, Edwards began his work with an exploration of true virtue, *not* with a critique of natural virtue. An assessment of so-called secondary virtue appears in the third chapter of his book, and a good portion of the text articulates ways in which natural virtue is often disguised as true virtue. So what, exactly, is the nature of *true* virtue?

Edwards defined true virtue as a "benevolence to being in general."[2] More specifically, he characterized virtue as "that consent, propensity and union of heart to being in general, which is immediately exercised in a

---

2   Jonathan Edwards, *The Nature of True Virtue* (Ann Arbor: University of Michigan Press, 1960), 3.

general good will."[3] While the language of a "good will" may lead us to think of Kant's subsequent deontological ethic, Edwards is remembered as an early American source for more teleological or consequentialist approaches. Writing in the twentieth century, noted ethicist William K. Frankena concluded that this essay by Edwards "was the beginning of a tradition of teleological and utilitarian thinking which strongly opposed the deontological intuitionism prevailing in American ethics in the nineteenth century."[4] At first it may be difficult to follow Frankena's point. Benevolence is a desire for the good of another, but that in itself hardly makes for utilitarianism. Jonathan Edwards employed the terminology of benevolence in exceedingly aesthetic, almost transcendent ways. Benevolence to being in general is an ontological reverence well before it filters down to a practical concern for creating the good. Still, the general trajectory of reasoning among *The Nature of True Virtue* opened a path for more worldly calculations of benevolence.

The lineage of thought that followed Edwards and his essay is instructive. Not only were there several generations that refined (or, according to some, distorted) his ethic. There were also decades of scholarship that evaluated the drift of this legacy. The common interpretation places Jonathan Edwards at the head and Edwards Amasa Park (1808–1900) at the end of a tradition known variously as the New Divinity or New England Theology. In 1907 Frank Hugh Foster offered the first major appraisal of this movement in a comprehensive study titled, *A Genetic History of the New England Theology.* Writing just after the tradition had faded, Foster emphasized the continuities of thought within the movement, hence the explicit reference to a "genetic" consistency through the years.

Foster acknowledged now-established patterns of change, such as the shift from theological determinism to a conception of freedom regarding the will. Yet he also stressed that the New England understanding of virtue remained basically Edwardsean in its insistence upon a benevolence

---

3   Edwards, 3.
4   Frankena's remark is a major point in his foreword to *The Nature of True Virtue* (Ann Arbor: University of Michigan Press, 1960), viii.

to general being. Later observers would take issue with Foster. Many saw quite a distinction between the virtue of Jonathan Edwards and the almost-utilitarian theories of some descendants. Frank Foster was perhaps the first scholar educated within the New England tradition to possess some independence before assessing the movement. Even then, he was sufficiently rooted in the grand old school of thought that his judgment cannot be considered entirely objective (if that is ever possible). Foster attempted to preserve the spirit of the movement, while honestly facing its lethargy as the twentieth century opened.[5]

Reverence for Jonathan Edwards has always seemed to find new expressions as the generations unfold. One contemporary retrieval of Edwards takes place within the movement known as "New Calvinism."[6] This rather diverse phenomenon among today's Evangelicalism seeks to make the puritan tradition real, even fashionable. Edwards serves as a kind of patron saint for the cause.

Sadly, Jonathan Edwards also receives attention for less inspiring reasons. In addition to more charitable treatments, many are examining his relationship with Atlantic slavery. During the nineteenth and twentieth centuries, theologians and church historians debated the ideas of Edwards and gave little energy to the fact that he "owned" human beings. Near the turn of the millennium, this issue drew closer scrutiny. How could such an honored and insightful intellectual participate in America's most notorious abuse? What are the facts of the matter? Did Edwards ever explain himself? How did Edwards square his behavior as one who bought and sold people with the idea of "true virtue"?

This last question is open to wide-ranging conjecture. Historians in general have focused on previously underreported realities and less on rationale. Craig Steven Wilder's 2013 study, *Ebony and Ivy: Race, Slavery,*

---

5   Frank Hugh Foster, *A Genetic History of the New England Theology* (Chicago: University of Chicago Press, 1907).

6   An accessible tour of this movement is found in Collin Hansen, *Young, Restless, Reformed: A Journalist's Journey with the New Calvinists* (Wheaton, Illinois: Crossway Books, 2008).

and the Troubled History of America's Universities has furthered scholarship that is finally willing to confront connections between prestigious eastern colleges and universities and slavery-laced economies.[7] There have been academic conferences and localized fact-finding efforts devoted to uncovering the ways early American higher education benefitted from slave labor, bequests generated from slavery, and the personal presence of enslaved people on campus. However, defining a worldview that attempted to justify such behavior remains incomplete. For starters, few who benefitted from slavery as business leaders and educators felt the need to defend their practices. Yet those who specifically addressed questions of right and wrong invite scrutiny. How did they rationalize their abuse?

According to the best scholarship available, Jonathan Edwards "owned" several human beings throughout his lifetime. Records show that he claimed ownership of a person named Joseph, as well as someone named Lee. He "purchased" a woman named Venus in 1731, and the inventory of his estate (1758) lists a young person named Titus.[8] It appears that Edwards accepted a fairly common belief that continuation of the slave trade was wrong but that the practice of slavery was not automatically so. Kenneth Minkema has stated that Edwards found slavery to be "a necessary evil that served some positive good in the natural order that God had decreed."[9] This may be, and such a conclusion reinforces the notion that teleological ethical cultures often rationalize abuse by pointing to some necessary evil. But, in the case of Jonathan Edwards, there might have been an even more subtle self-justification.

The ethereal, even aesthetic way in which Edwards spoke of being tended to drive a wedge between the world that exists and the world to come. He may even have longed for a time when inequities will disappear, but he was willing to accept them in an imperfect world. Of course, he

---

7   Craig Steven Wilder, *Ebony & Ivy: Race, Slavery, and the Troubled History of America's Universities* (New York: Bloomsbury Press, 2013).

8   Kenneth P. Minkema, "Jonathan Edwards on Slavery and the Slave Trade," *The William and Mary Quarterly* 54, no. 4 (October 1997): 825.

9   Minkema, 825.

was one who benefitted from such imperfection, and there did not seem to be much troubling of conscience around this particular fact. The rationale offered by Edwards does not in any manner soften his abuse of privilege, but it does place his behavior within an eschatological context.[10]

Samuel Hopkins and Disinterested Benevolence

The successors of Jonathan Edwards inherited significant burden when it came to explaining the relationship between "true virtue" and slavery. Samuel Hopkins was perhaps the primary heir of the tradition, and, overall, he acquitted himself quite well. Yet the rather admirable record Hopkins left regarding social reform came with a price. Subsequent scholars have debated his faithfulness to the theological legacy of Edwards.

Samuel Hopkins (1721–1803) was born in Waterbury, Connecticut, and died in Newport, Rhode Island. He was graduated from Yale College in 1741 and served as a pastor in western Massachusetts. He moved to Newport in 1770 and developed most of his social principles within this urban (and urbane) context.

Like Edwards, Hopkins has received several different readings that span the generations.[11] We should not be surprised to observe that Foster's 1907 treatment of Hopkins stressed the continuities between his moral theory and that of Edwards. Later scholars saw in Hopkins a significant departure from the master. Speaking during the days of pre-Revolutionary soul searching, Samuel Hopkins offered his analysis in 1773: *An Inquiry into the Nature of True Holiness*. Here he attempted to extend the Edwardsean tradition, but he did introduce variations on established themes. First, he transformed "benevolence to being" into a love for God and neighbor. Second, he emphasized a polarity between self-love and sacrificial love.

These modifications have come down to us as a signature concern for "disinterested benevolence." When establishing a divine criterion for this

---

10 This point is made by Kenneth P. Minkema in "Johnathan Edwards's Defense of Slavery," *Massachusetts Historical Review: Race and Slavery* 4 (2002): 41.

11 See, for instance, Oliver D. Crisp and Douglas Sweeney, eds., *After Jonathan Edwards: The Courses of the New England Theology*.

practice, Hopkins wrote that God's love to humanity was "in the highest degree, disinterested benevolence, as it was love to enemies; and such a regard for their good, as to lead him to be willing to take their misery on himself, and bear it all, that they might escape, and live forever."[12] Further, Hopkins suggested the self-denying qualities of this benevolence by stating that "the excellency of it is owned to consist very much in its being in such a striking degree *disinterested* love and goodness."[13] The challenge came with interpreting how closely those transformed by this divine gift may live in a like manner. This question is debatable to our day, but the standard remained a part of the theology Samuel Hopkins propagated.

By 1793, he could say that "disinterested benevolence is pleased with the publick interest, the greatest good and happiness of the whole."[14] Such language came awfully close to theological utilitarianism, and later critics accused Hopkins of turning the sublime reflection found throughout Edwards into a calculating legalism. This withering analysis characterized the view of Joseph Haroutunian, who, in 1932, wrote a landmark text, *Piety Versus Moralism: The Passing of the New England Theology.* It was perhaps fitting that Haroutunian published his study the same year Reinhold Niebuhr released his epoch-making work, *Moral Man and Immoral Society.* Just as Niebuhr castigated early-twentieth-century liberalism for its moral pretense, Haroutunian found fault with Frank Foster's optimistic reading of New England theology. Where Foster documented faithful linkages, Haroutunian charted the demise of a tradition. He wrote: "Hopkins impoverished the Calvinistic 'glory of God' beyond recognition. He had drunk too deeply of the humanitarian spirit, which was reducing Calvinism to a formal legalism by forcing it to think in its own terms, though

---

12 Samuel Hopkins, *An Inquiry into the Nature of True Holiness. With an Appendix* (Newport, Rhode Island: Solomon Southwick, 1773), 50.

13 Hopkins, 50.

14 Samuel Hopkins, *The System of Doctrines, Contained in Divine Revelation, Explained and Defended*, Vol. 1 (Boston: Isaiah Thomas and Ebenezer T. Andrews, 1793), 547.

not toward its own conclusions."[15] From Haroutunian's perspective, Hopkins trivialized the transcendental love of being and made it a concern for public welfare.

Such critiques, though nearly a century old now, should be taken seriously. The refreshingly acerbic tone of some theology from the 1930s warned a world on the precipice of demagogic folly. However, this angle of vision also overlooked other, absolutely critical, moral dimensions. For example, the index of Haroutunian's classic does not include the words "slave" or "slavery," and the text exhibits a notable disregard for the issue. These observations may seem like inappropriate twenty-first-century judgment. For decades scholarship traced the history of theological ideas without much reference to social context, but Haroutunian's omission is particularly instructive. His doctrinal focus viewed Samuel Hopkins with considerable suspicion. Yet in terms of social justice, Hopkins may have been one of the few to enhance New England theology's integrity.

Before arriving in Newport, Rhode Island, Samuel Hopkins displayed little commitment to end the slave trade or slavery. There is evidence that an African American woman lived as a servant among the Hopkins household in Great Barrington, Massachusetts. Not only had his mentor (Edwards) "owned" people. Others of the same theological tradition participated in such abuse, though Jonathan Edwards Jr. did develop an antislavery position.[16] Over time, however, Samuel Hopkins was probably the best-known heir of the elder Edwards to come out strongly against slavery, and it may be that the same shifts in theological emphasis derided by Joseph Haroutunian guided Hopkins and his maturing witness.

Newport, Rhode Island, was a cosmopolitan center for trade in all manner of things—and people. When Samuel Hopkins left his simple environs of western Massachusetts to serve the First Congregational Church of Newport, he saw for himself the commercialized brutality of

---

15 Joseph Haroutunian, *Piety Versus Moralism: The Passing of the New England Theology* (New York: Henry Holt and Company, 1932), 83.

16 Joseph A. Conforti, *Samuel Hopkins and the New Divinity Movement* (Grand Rapids, Michigan: William B. Eerdmans Publishing Company, 1981), 126–27.

buying and selling human beings. The combination of a developing ethical theory and the inexcusably wretched excess in Newport drove Hopkins to speak out.

Additionally, we must note that most leaders of the movement embraced by Hopkins were not privileged simply by their association with Yale. While New Haven served as the theological locus for their preparation, many came from families of common social status. Many also returned to the backcountry once credentialed for ministry.[17] Contrary to this pattern, Hopkins did inherit a more prominent standing, but he embodied the tradition that united theological rigor with simple living. By the 1770s he was bound to clash with Newport's refined moral compromising.

This he did, and in 1776 Samuel Hopkins took his case to the very seat of revolutionary America—the Continental Congress. *A Dialogue Concerning the Slavery of the Africans* became legendary. In this piece, dedicated to the founders of the Republic, Hopkins argued for the elimination of slavery. His overall theme matched some other appeals: a new nation, constructed from resistance to abusive power, could not retain an institution that exemplified the abuse of power. But, the particularities of his argument were pure Samuel Hopkins.

Of course, the theme of "benevolence" is woven through the *Dialogue*. Yet the manner in which Hopkins cut at the root of self-interest and rationalization is most striking. He did not accept the objection that emancipation would be imprudent and detrimental for the nation as a whole. To this claim Hopkins responded that resistance had more to do with "selfish motives, and a backwardness to give up what you unrighteously retain."[18] He added that there was "no insurmountable difficulty, but that which lies in your own heart."[19] So much for rationalizing abuse as a necessary evil.

---

17 See especially, "The Connecticut Background," in Joseph A. Conforti, *Samuel Hopkins and the New Divinity Movement*, 9–22.

18 Samuel Hopkins, *A Dialogue Concerning the Slavery of the Africans; Shewing It to be the Duty and Interest of the American States to Emancipate All Their African Slaves* (Norwich, Vermont: Judah P. Spooner, 1776), 39.

19 Hopkins, 39.

In the middle 1780s, Hopkins prepared an essay that appeared in two installments among the *Providence Gazette and Country Journal*. This piece, under the name Crito and released in October of 1787, returned to principles of benevolence, but once again it challenged others to find any credible justification for slavery. With a rather taunting tone, Hopkins wrote: "It is earnestly to be desired therefore, if this be possible, that some able, disinterested advocate for the slave trade, if such a one can be found, would step forth, and do it."[20] He even conceded that he would hear an "interested" advocate for slavery "shew it to be just and benevolent, if they can."[21] Hopkins denied that such an argument could be made.

These rhetorical strategies reveal much about the ethic of Samuel Hopkins. He was by no means without fault. As late as the middle 1770s he still dabbled in colonization plans for people of African descent.[22] Yet his indebtedness to Jonathan Edwards and linkage to later teleological thinkers must be qualified. The teleological or consequentialist ethic could be pressed to rationalize oppressive systems. After all, the greater good sometimes required acceptance of regrettable wrong or even unavoidable evil. However, the powerful seldom placed themselves within the community of those who were sacrificed for this so-called greater good. Samuel Hopkins, with his emphasis on "disinterestedness," did exactly that. He called out the selfish justifications of abusers. This fact made Hopkins a unique and more admirable bearer of the teleological ethic. His successors would not leave such a legacy.

The Privilege of Defining Benevolence

February of 2017 witnessed a particularly striking university decision regarding how Americans remember slavery. Yale President Peter Salovey announced that the institution's Calhoun College would receive a new

---

20 *Providence Gazette and Country Journal*, Vol. XXIV, October 6, 1787, no. 1240, Page 1.

21 *Providence Gazette and Country Journal,* October 6, 1787, Page 1.

22 Edmund S. Morgan, *The Gentle Puritan: A Life of Ezra Stiles, 1727–1795* (New Haven: Yale University Press, 1962), 451.

name. The change would honor Grace Murray Hopper, a gifted mathematician and computer scientist. The catalyst for this decision was John C. Calhoun's proslavery views. Calhoun (1782–1850), from South Carolina and a Yale graduate of 1804, later became synonymous with an energetic defense of slavery. President Salovey described the Calhoun legacy as that of "a white supremacist and national leader who passionately promoted slavery as a 'positive good.'"[23] This characterization of Calhoun's ideology is no accident.

The reference to some positive good is derived from a notorious Calhoun speech, delivered before Congress on February 6, 1837. While criticizing northern leaders, he thundered: "I hold that, in the present state of civilization, where two races of different origin and distinguished by colour, and other physical differences, as well as intellectual, are brought together, the relation now existing in the slaveholding states between the two is, instead of an evil, a good—a positive good."[24]

Many will interpret the Yale decision as simply one more example of the ways prestigious universities are confronting their past entanglements with slavery, but there is much more to this story. In some respects, Calhoun is an easy target. Thankfully, the strategy of promoting injustice as a positive good finds few supporters today. We might wonder, though, if the decision would have been the same had Calhoun accepted slavery as a necessary evil. The distinction is not without a difference. It is one thing to aim for a communal good and acknowledge wrong as an unavoidable byproduct. It is something else entirely to proclaim that the abuse is, in itself, good. This distinction was not overlooked by President Salovey. He even contrasted Calhoun's view with other nineteenth-century compromisers who "treated slavery as a 'necessary evil.'"[25] The president's

---

23 Peter Salovey, "Decision on the Name of Calhoun College," Yale University, Office of the President, Saturday, February 11, 2017.

24 John C. Calhoun, *Speeches of John C. Calhoun. Delivered in the Congress of the United States from 1811 to the Present Time* (New York: Harper & Brothers, 1843), 225.

25 Salovey, "Decision on the Name of Calhoun College," February 11, 2017.

terminology and logic reveal much, perhaps unintentionally, about the Yale tradition in moral philosophy.

While both Jonathan Edwards and Samuel Hopkins are identified with the principles dominant at Yale during the eighteenth century, the culture of teleological thinking took on a more formal institutional identity during the American Revolution. Among this narrative, Ezra Stiles served as a transitional figure. Stiles (1727–1795) was born in North Haven, Connecticut, and died in New Haven. During his life he personified the gentleman scholar. He was graduated from Yale in 1746 and served as a tutor at the college from 1749–1755. In 1755 he became the pastor of Newport, Rhode Island's Second Congregational Church and in 1778 assumed the presidency of Yale.[26]

The life of Ezra Stiles reminds us that terms such as "liberal" and "conservative" do not hold up well under historical scrutiny. Stiles was, in many ways, a person of liberal sensibilities. He was urbane and sophisticated, and his theological views were moderately opposed to the more straightforward doctrines of New England's revivalist community. For instance, Samuel Hopkins represented the "New Light" movement, which was really an attempt to revive more conservative doctrinal commitments. In contrast, Ezra Stiles embodied a cultured, "Old Light" establishment— a measured and temperate base of power that was more flexible about drawing distinctions between the church and the world.

The contrast was especially apparent among the two congregations Hopkins and Stiles served in Newport. The Second Congregational Church of Ezra Stiles had broken away from the First Church in 1729, when the latter was led by a conservative pastor.[27] This meant that Stiles, who arrived in Newport before Hopkins, enjoyed a large, liberal, and relatively elite congregation. When Hopkins came in 1769/1770 he stepped into a smaller, more conservative body. It also meant that Ezra Stiles

---

26 Perhaps the most durable and thorough treatment of Stiles is Edmund S. Morgan's 1962 study, *The Gentle Puritan: A Life of Ezra Stiles, 1727–1795.*

27 Joseph A. Conforti, *Samuel Hopkins and the New Divinity Movement*, 99.

worked among those with great resources, while many served by Hopkins were of modest means.

The difference between Samuel Hopkins and Ezra Stiles was as much about class as it was about theology. Both were from backgrounds of privilege, but Hopkins embraced the simple focus of his ecclesiastical community. Stiles was at ease among the upper class. This difference was bound to harbor implications for social issues. The Newport of Samuel Hopkins fueled his developing antislavery stance. Ezra Stiles possessed a less troubled conscience. In fact, Stiles saw nothing wrong with participating in slavery soon after arriving in Newport. He traded a hogshead of rum for a young boy taken from the African coast.[28] As interpreted by Edmund Morgan:

> It might be supposed that a man who made a religion of morality would have found something wrong with the slave trade. To Stiles's discredit, as yet he did not. He was no more drawn to novelty in morals than in science, and though it would have been no great novelty to condemn slavery, few people in New England did. It was not uncommon for ministers to own slaves. His father did, and so did Jonathan Edwards.[29]

Years later, Stiles freed the young man, but the record shows that he then entered into a contract of indenture with the Stiles family.[30] This enigmatic relationship Stiles bore with slavery invites many questions, and these questions are not easily answered.

The personal diary of Ezra Stiles has given historians a sweeping collection of daily observations but remains a cryptic source for deeper consideration. For instance, an entry dated May 25, 1772, states: "Conversed

---

28 Morgan, *The Gentle Puritan: A Life of Ezra Stiles, 1727–1795*, 125.

29 Morgan, 125.

30 Ezra Stiles, *The Literary Diary of Ezra Stiles*, DD, LLD, Edited Under the Authority of the Corporation of Yale University by Franklin Bowditch Dexter, MA, Volume II, March 14, 1776–December 31, 1781 (New York: Charles Scribner's Sons, 1901), 272. Ibid., Volume III, January 1, 1782–May 6, 1795, 51.

with Capt. Balch on *disinterested Benevolence*."[31] There is no indication of the perspective Stiles expressed regarding this principle, but we might note two unspoken pieces of context. First, this conversation took place one year before formal publication of *An Inquiry into the Nature of True Holiness* by Samuel Hopkins. Second, the "Capt. Balch" mentioned may have been affiliated with the First Congregational Church, where Hopkins had recently become pastor. Records indicate a Balch family as members of First Church during the 1760s and 1770s.[32]

Stiles was called to the presidency of Yale in 1778 and thereafter made his personal theological and social proclivities a part of that institution's culture. He served in this capacity until his death in 1795. As late as November 22, 1789, Stiles mentioned hearing a sermon on disinterested benevolence. It was delivered in chapel by a Mr. Austin from the text of Philippians 2:4, an instruction related to the self-denying and self-emptying ministry of Jesus Christ.[33]

However, the most remarkable and telling reference to disinterested benevolence offered by Ezra Stiles may be the one that figures prominently in his 1783 address, *The United States Elevated to Glory and Honor.* This lengthy ode to the promise of post-revolutionary America included a sentimental tribute to George Washington. Speaking directly to the legendary figure, Stiles said: "There is a glory in thy *disinterested benevolence*, which the greatest characters would purchase, if possible, at the expense of worlds, and which may excite indeed their emulation, but cannot be felt by the VENAL GREAT—who think every thing, even *virtue* and true glory, may be bought and sold, and trace our every action

---

31 Stiles, *The Literary Diary of Ezra Stiles*, Vol. I, January 1, 1769—March 13, 1776, 238.

32 James N. Arnold, *Vital Record of Rhode Island, 1636–1850, First Series, Births, Marriages and Deaths, A Family Register for the People*, Vol. VIII, Episcopal and Congregational (Providence, R.I.: Narragansett Historical Publishing Company, 1896), 401 and 412.

33 Stiles, *The Literary Diary of Ezra Stiles*, Vol. III, January 1, 1782–May 6, 1795, 371.

to motives terminating in *self*."[34] This language reflects the mythology that circulated around Washington, the great gentleman farmer. He was, according to legend, the American Cincinnatus who put down his plow to lead a necessary war—eventually exchanging his sword for the familiar plowshare. This language also says something about the notion of benevolence idealized by Ezra Stiles.

We might conclude that, for Stiles, disinterested benevolence was ultimately a kind of *noblesse oblige*, the civic-mindedness of powerful people. Late in life he lent his prestige to a Connecticut antislavery society, but his overall understanding of benevolence differed from that of Samuel Hopkins.[35] To Hopkins disinterested benevolence was a raw wariness of power. To Stiles it was a rather self-congratulatory wielding of power—for some purported good. It is no wonder that Hopkins and Stiles never really reconciled their respective understandings of Atlantic slavery. Like other venerated leaders who could not embrace a fully antislavery consciousness, Ezra Stiles could not get over his privilege.

Utility at Yale

The waning years of the Stiles administration at Yale saw the addition of a well-known text on ethics among the curriculum. William Paley's *Moral and Political Philosophy* was introduced to Yale students in 1791.[36] Yet the circumstances of Paley's entry into Yale are murky. The literary diary that Ezra Stiles kept mentions Paley as a figure of study in the summer of 1792 and during the last years of his presidency, but we can hardly attribute this

---

34 Ezra Stiles D.D. and Reiner Smolinski, eds., "The United States Elevated to Glory and Honor" (1783), Electronic Texts in American Studies, Paper 41, 42, http://digitalcommons.unl.eduetas/41.

35 Morgan, *The Gentle Puritan: A Life of Ezra Stiles, 1727–1795*, 452.

36 Wilson Smith, *Professors and Public Ethics: Studies of Northern Moral Philosophers before the Civil War* (Ithaca, New York: Cornell University Press, 1956), 47. Louis Franklin Snow, "The College Curriculum in the United States" (PhD diss., Columbia University, 1907), 91. "Memoranda: Yale College," June 17, 1791 (cited in Morgan, *The Gentle Puritan*, 391).

period's reign of teleological thinking at Yale to Paley.[37] When Ezra Stiles died, Paley's influence at the college was just getting traction.

For generations, observers of American higher education have noted 1795 not so much because it marked the passing of Stiles but because of the supposed contrast in leadership that ensued at Yale. The new president was Timothy Dwight. According to longstanding interpretation, Stiles was a genteel and frail doctor who lost his touch and his ability to inspire young adults. Tales of institutional malaise and student misconduct were legion. Lyman Beecher, who studied under both presidents, considered Dwight's coming a godsend: "Before he came college was in a most ungodly state. The college church was almost extinct. Most of the students were skeptical, and rowdies were plenty."[38] It is not difficult to imagine this scenario, given the way Stiles moved in nuanced and deliberate ways. Timothy Dwight was known for more forthright proclamation and administration, but we should be careful before concluding that Dwight was a scholar after the fashion of Samuel Hopkins.

Timothy Dwight (1752–1817) was born in Northampton, Massachusetts, the grandson of Jonathan Edwards. He was graduated from Yale in 1769. Two years later Dwight became a tutor at his alma mater. After a stint as an army chaplain during the Revolution, Dwight returned to Northampton and pursued various forms of public service and farming. In 1783 he became the pastor of a congregation in Greenfield Hill, Connecticut. He was called to succeed Ezra Stiles as president of Yale during the summer of 1795.[39]

The habit of contrasting Stiles and Dwight regarding religious orthodoxy and vigor has been challenged in more recent years. For example,

---

37 Stiles, *The Literary Diary of Ezra Stiles*, Volume III, January 1, 1782–May 6, 1795, 469 and 513.

38 Lyman Beecher, *The Autobiography of Lyman Beecher*, ed. Barbara M. Cross, Vol. 1 (Cambridge, Massachusetts: Harvard University Press, 1961), 27.

39 Many consider the biography of Dwight written by Charles E. Cunningham the authoritative work. See Charles E. Cunningham, *Timothy Dwight, 1752–1817* (New York: The Macmillan Company, 1942). See also Kenneth Silverman, *Timothy Dwight* (New York: Twayne Publishers, Inc., 1969).

Edmund Morgan granted that the two men were of different temperament but equally competent as college presidents. He wrote: "It is time, I think, to reopen the case of Stiles vs. Dwight and to judge the two men, not by what students thought of them at a particular time, not by what they thought of each other, and not by what old men remembered of them, but by their actual achievements."[40] We, too, might reopen the comparison—but with a special concern for moral philosophy, as well as practice.

If regard for William Paley serves as one indicator of the commonalities and distinctions between the two presidents, we must come down on the side of continuity. The leadership of Yale, like many others, could not endorse all that Paley promoted, but he remained important to the overall ethical culture in New Haven. As Bruce Kuklick reminded us: "Paley's texts were standard under Dwight and contributed to the notion that God's concern was human happiness."[41] The rub, of course, was defining the nature of human happiness and how it might look among a wider society.

From a theoretical perspective, Dwight's posthumously published *Theology Explained and Defended in a Series of Sermons* is critical. This massive work was drawn from a collection of addresses preached to undergraduates. The president organized his sermons so that by preaching one per week each student would hear them all over four years of study.[42] It is no surprise that William Paley appears in prominent places among these discourses, especially in the third volume. Here Dwight addressed the law of God as it relates to the second great commandment (love to people). He gave this sermon the heading, "Utility the Foundation of Virtue" and wrote "that a disposition voluntarily employed in doing good, is productive of more Personal and Public happiness, than any other can

---

40 Edmund S. Morgan, *American Heroes: Profiles of Men and Women Who Shaped Early America* (New York: W. W. Norton & Company, 2009), 194.

41 Bruce Kuklick, *Churchmen and Philosophers: From Jonathan Edwards to John Dewey*, 96.

42 Timothy Dwight, *Theology Explained and Defended, in a Series of Sermons*, Vol. I (Middletown, Connecticut: Clark and Lyman, 1818), xxxiii–xxxiv.

be."[43] This linkage between happiness and utility so closely resembled Paley's thought that we might easily conflate the ethic of Timothy Dwight and the English moralist. There were differences.

Dwight held that human calculations of utility were not necessarily identical with divine determination of value. The president insisted that God was the ultimate judge and so sought to distance himself from more secular kinds of utilitarianism.[44] He even challenged William Paley outright regarding the morality of lying. Though Paley concluded that certain forms of deception may be acceptable, Dwight found this hard to support. The president went so far as to claim that Paley erred by arguing that the end justifies the means.[45]

Timothy Dwight embodied the qualified affirmation of William Paley expressed by many New England divines. While not wanting to accept a crass consequentialism, teachers like Dwight did end up endorsing a theologically determined "utility" as the foundation of virtue. How later generations employed this framework reveals the degree to which moral theory, in general, was bent to rationalize predetermined convictions.

For instance, this wielding of moral theory to support existing perspectives is noticeable in one of Timothy Dwight's star pupils, Nathaniel William Taylor (1786–1858). Taylor was born in New Milford, Connecticut, and died in New Haven. He was graduated from Yale in 1807 and in 1812 became the pastor of New Haven's First Church. In 1822 he was appointed the Dwight Professor of Didactic Theology at Yale's new "Theological Department." For several decades, Nathaniel William Taylor's name was synonymous with a particular form of the New England theology.[46]

---

43 Timothy Dwight, *Theology Explained and Defended in a Series of Sermons*, Vol. III (New Haven, Connecticut: S. Converse, 1823), 150.

44 Dwight, 159.

45 Dwight, 496.

46 Sidney Mead's enduring biography remains the standard for treatments of Taylor. See Sidney Earl Mead, *Nathaniel William Taylor, 1786–1858: A Connecticut Liberal* (Chicago: The University of Chicago Press, 1942).

Taylor was a protégé of Dwight in an exceedingly specific manner. As a student he embraced Dwight's understanding of "utility" so closely that he earned his mentor's unique praise. Later, Taylor recalled one pivotal exchange:

> In my Senior year, I read as an exercise before Dr. Dwight, an argument on the question—"Is virtue founded in utility?"—a question in which he always felt a peculiar interest. To those who preceded me he said, "Oh, you do not understand the question," but when I had finished my argument, he remarked with great emphasis,—"That's right," and added some other commendatory remarks which, to say the least, were adapted to put a young man's modesty to rather a severe test.[47]

As the years progressed, Nathaniel William Taylor blended his teleological ethic with the theme of God's moral government. For decades his teaching developed a codification of the way civil government and its laws reflected the design of God.

Following Taylor's death, his lectures were organized and published under the title, *Lectures on the Moral Government of God*. Quite early among this two-volume work the issue of prioritizing moral obligation is addressed. Taylor wrote that certain precepts may require exceptions, "in view of the great end of all action on the part of moral beings."[48] Here he cited William Paley and, in a note, clarified his comment by asserting that "the greatest good is to be done, in all cases, notwithstanding the unqualified language of particular precepts."[49] This dependence on Paley may not seem unusual, but the seventh lecture posed a more ominous consideration.

---

47 William B. Sprague, *Annals of the American Pulpit*, Vol. II (New York: Robert Carter & Brothers, 1859), 162.

48 Nathaniel William Taylor, *Lectures on the Moral Government of God*, Vol. I (New York: Clark, Austin & Smith, 1859), 58.

49 Taylor, 58.

Among seemingly innocuous discussion of the way government is to protect life, liberty, and property, Nathaniel Taylor inserted a revealing footnote. He insisted that there were qualifications to these rights and stated that no one

> has, as some modern fanatical moralists and politicians maintain, an absolute right to either life, or liberty, or property, i.e., in all cases or circumstances. When the public good demands the sacrifice of either or of all these blessings, whether on account of crime or for the defense of the state, or for the greatest public good in any way, the surrender must be made. The state has a right to it, and the subject has no opposing right.[50]

We cannot read this as a carefully guarded statement. Taylor left the door wide open for a consequentialist ethic that disregarded rights out of some purported reverence for "the greatest public good in any way." This comprehensive rationale invites a serious question. Did Nathaniel William Taylor employ his theory to justify the violation of human rights when considering contemporary issues? Sadly, he did.

For years historians have mined the minutes of student literary societies to read about nineteenth-century college culture and social attitudes. The minutes of the Yale Theological Department Rhetorical Society reveal much. This organization was led by a standing committee of five students, but the president of the society was none other than Nathaniel William Taylor. Meetings were held weekly, and procedure typically unfolded through an opening prayer, various reports, and structured debate of a previously selected question. At the close of each debate, the president (Taylor) offered his opinion regarding the question, often accompanied by lengthy rationale.[51]

Of critical importance were the debates held on October 19 and October 26, 1842. The question: "Does the greatest good of the greatest number

---

50 Taylor, 147.

51 John T. Wayland, *The Theological Department in Yale College: 1822–1858* (New York & London: Garland Publishing, Inc., 1987), 291–97.

justify the further continuance of slavery at the South?" The minutes for the discussion of October 26 record that, "In view of his present knowledge the President [Taylor] was rather of the opinion that the greatest good of the greatest numbers justified the further continuance of the system."[52] The question was revisited on November 22, 1843. The president of the society stated that, "Perhaps it may."[53] As late as December 6, 1848, the same question was debated. The president voiced his affirmative opinion, and the student members sustained him.[54]

Though the argument and conclusions of these meetings are telling, the process of discourse is equally striking. Not all literary societies were organized with a principal professor as primary adjudicator. Yet here Nathaniel William Taylor, the faculty member most responsible for helping students develop ethical ideas, deployed enormous power within these debates. Over the course of several years we can chart the way Taylor's teleological rationale for slavery eventually carried the day. Not long before his death, Nathaniel William Taylor endorsed an antislavery position, but for the majority of his career he sought to legitimate slavery as a justifiable institution.

Utilitarianism in the Old South

It would be easy to pin all responsibility for rationalizing slavery on privileged clergy, but the story is more complicated. In fact, intellectuals of all religious sensitivities and those of no particular religious commitment often applied utilitarian criteria to defend injustice. One of the most striking examples is the life of Thomas Cooper, a radical thinker from England who became a secular advocate for slavery and resident of South Carolina. Cooper (1759–1839) was born in Westminster and educated at Oxford, though he failed to complete his degree. An insatiable intellectual curiosity, coupled with a cantankerous personality, led him to study law and

---

52 Folder 3 (Secretary's Book: Minutes) of RU 448, Rhetorical Society, Yale College, Records.

53 Folder 3.

54 Folder 3.

immerse himself in philosophy and chemistry. He became friends with the English scientist Joseph Priestley and developed a rather strident penchant for metaphysical materialism.[55]

Cooper and Priestley both removed to the United States in 1794, and the former sought to combine his scientific views with political theory. Philosophical materialism claimed that the very nature of reality was material and could be explored in almost mechanistic ways. It stood opposed to both the idealism of the Northeast and the Scottish Realism of the emerging "West." To a great extent, Cooper fit the profile of a philosophical materialist whose new home (Northumberland, Pennsylvania) put him close to the materialism prominent in postrevolutionary Philadelphia. Like many others of the time, Cooper eventually traveled south with this perspective. In 1820 he became professor of chemistry in South Carolina College (now the University of South Carolina). He was elevated to the presidency of this institution not long after arriving and emerged as the standard-bearer for both calculating scientific reasoning and utilitarian ethics in the Old South.[56]

Temperamentally, Cooper was the opposite of those apologists for slavery who exuded traditional piety. He was, by all accounts, openly antagonistic toward the clergy, and he was not an orthodox supporter of organized religion. Cooper personified the most advanced, "objective," and forward-looking values of the academy. He was also a cold and abrasive defender of slavery.

During the 1820s and 1830s, Cooper even argued for the prerogative of states against the federal government. He became, in the words of Dumas Malone, "the academic philosopher of state rights and, as a

---

55 A milestone biography of Thomas Cooper was adapted from the 1923 PhD dissertation by Dumas Malone: *The Public Life of Thomas Cooper, 1783–1839* (New Haven: Yale University Press, 1926).

56 Woodbridge Riley's classic 1907 study contains a revealing chapter on the materialism of Cooper. I. Woodbridge Riley, *American Philosophy: The Early Schools*, 407–20.

teacher and writer, exerted a profound and lasting influence."[57] By 1826, Cooper codified his theory in his *Lectures on the Elements of Political Economy*. Near the very close of this text, he wrote:

> The only safeguard in our confederacy, is the absolute inviolability of state sovereignty and state rights; which no state ought to suffer for a moment to be submitted to, controlled, or construed, or decided on, or in any way meddled with, by any tribunal whatever—by any power on earth but the State itself; reserving to itself, not merely the implied, but the expressed and declared right of withdrawing peaceably from the Union, whenever circumstances may render it expedient, or the persevering injustice of a majority, may render it necessary to do so.[58]

Thus, more than thirty years before the American Civil War, Thomas Cooper was planting the seeds for secession.

This argument accompanied Cooper's contempt for the inconvenient revolutionary doctrine that all are created equal. Was Cooper really prepared to say that the words of Thomas Jefferson, a friend, were wrong? He was. To the notion that all people are born free, equal, and independent, Cooper replied: "I know of no sense in which this ever was, or is, or can, or will be true."[59] For him, rights are not inherent—to be protected *by* government—but the sole prerogative *of* government, particularly state government: "That which society refuses to acknowledge or sanction, is not a right; it has no character of a right."[60] So how was society to be ordered, according to Thomas Cooper? Not surprisingly, the only operative way to create appropriate government was according to "public expedience,

---

57 See the entry by Dumas Malone in: Allen Johnson and Dumas Malone, eds., *Dictionary of American Biography*, Vol. IV (New York: Charles Scribner's Sons, 1943), 415.

58 Thomas Cooper, *Lectures on the Elements of Political Economy*, 2nd ed. (Columbia, South Carolina: M'Morris & Wilson, Printers, 1829), 365.

59 Cooper, 360.

60 Cooper, 362.

public utility, the greatest good of the greatest number considered in all the bearings of the rule adopted, and as a permanent law of the society."[61] This meant that those with political power decided who counted and who did not count.

In an essay on theories of education, Cooper made it plain that he considered political power a special privilege of those fit to rule. He declared: "We cannot help thinking that the root of the evil lies in UNIVERSAL SUFFRAGE. The right of voting, we conceive, is a right to be earned, before it is enjoyed."[62] This attitude was directed at a host of underrepresented people from many ethnic backgrounds. Yet Cooper's defense of white supremacy held a special place among his elitist philosophy. In an 1835 piece, Cooper maintained as a matter of scientific "fact" that people of African descent were inferior to white people. The American system of slavery was, for him, the best possible ordering of relationships between incompatible races and the best possible arrangement for both black and white people.[63]

As Daniel Kilbride wrote: "Slavery, he reasoned, was economically viable; it was principled because it provided for the good of the slave, who was the moral and mental inferior of the master race. But Cooper found slavery to be consistent with a modern and progressive philosophy. The peculiar institution, he believed, had a future in a world governed by utilitarian ethics."[64] This narrative does not prove that all utilitarian theories automatically led to racist conclusions, but a denial of natural or divinely bestowed rights did open the way for a cynical and self-serving calculation of good throughout the Old South. There were plenty of religious leaders who endorsed slavery as some supposedly benevolent institution, sanctioned by the Bible. Yet even those who took pride in their modern and secular thinking could find cover for oppression in utilitarian reasoning.

---

61 Cooper, 362.

62 Thomas Cooper, "Agrarian and Educational Systems," *Southern Review* VI (August 1830): 21.

63 Thomas Cooper, "Slavery," *Southern Literary Journal* 1 (November 1835): 189.

64 Daniel Kilbride, "Slavery and Utilitarianism: Thomas Cooper and the Mind of the Old South," *The Journal of Southern History* 59, no. 3 (August 1993), 475.

Organized Religion and Consequentialism in the Old South

Unorthodox moderns cannot be let off the hook when it comes to defending slavery, but the overall southern culture was perhaps more indebted to smooth and rhetorically gifted church folk for rationalizations. One example is the ecclesiastical and academic leadership of Virginia's William Andrew Smith (1802–1870). Born in Fredericksburg, Virginia, Smith lost both of his parents at an early age. He was supported by various people throughout the region and joined the Methodist Episcopal Church, becoming a preacher on a probationary basis in 1825. He was admitted to the Virginia Conference as a pastor in full connection during 1827. Smith served churches in Petersburg, Lynchburg, Richmond, and Norfolk, blossoming into a preacher of great renown. His homiletical skills and political clout enabled him to be a delegate at every General Conference of the Methodist Episcopal Church from 1832 through 1844.[65]

It was at the fateful General Conference of 1844 that the conflict over slavery came to a head. Most historians have focused on the dilemma facing the Methodist Episcopal Church regarding southern bishop James Andrew's connection with slavery, but a preceding debate at the 1844 gathering featured a lengthy defense of that institution by William Andrew Smith.

Francis Harding of the Baltimore Conference had been suspended by that body for failing to free enslaved people who were bound to him through marriage. Harding appealed to the General Conference, and William Andrew Smith acted in his defense. The detail and breadth of Smith's argument are telling. At first he dissected the various factors of the case— how Harding had been charged, the response of Harding to his home conference, what the civil law allowed or did not allow in Maryland, and

---

65 See the entry by Robert Emory Blackwell in Allen Johnson and Dumas Malone, eds., *Dictionary of American Biography*, Vol. 17 (New York: Charles Scribner's Sons, 1943), 361–62.

whether disciplinary procedure had been followed correctly. Then Smith's advocacy shifted toward a sweeping rationalization of slavery itself.[66]

The approach taken by Smith to excuse slavery reveals much and can be juxtaposed with his later, more systematic reasoning. Speaking to the gathered delegates of the General Conference, he intoned:

> I should say that while the Discipline deprecates the evil of slavery, it requires the members of the Church within those states to conform their action to the rules or laws of those states in which they live. This is assuming the doctrine that though slavery is an evil, and a great evil, it is not necessarily a sin. There's the other side of the question. And is it not clearly so? Now, we of the south take both sides of the question—it is a great evil, *it is not necessarily a sin*; and we ask no more of you. But we maintain that it is not a sin, and we demand this concession on your part.[67]

From the standpoint of ethical theory, this statement invites a question. Is the differentiation between evil and sin a distinction with or without a difference? Given the context of Smith's argument, it is difficult to know exactly how he hoped to split the terms. Overall he seemed to be suggesting that slavery was an unavoidable evil and that those who participated in the system were not automatically committing sin.

Smith *did* deny that slavery was "a great political and social blessing," but he also denied that southern Methodists took such ground.[68] His argument was perhaps best summed up when he said: "Now on this broad platform the southern Church stands:—Slavery is a great evil, but beyond our control; yet not necessarily a sin. We must then quietly submit to a necessity which we cannot control or remedy, endeavouring to carry the

---

66 Emory Stevens Bucke, ed., *History of Methodism*, Vol. 3 (New York: Abingdon Press, 1964), 52.

67 Robert Athow West, *Report of Debates in the General Conference of the Methodist Episcopal Church, Held in the City of New York, 1844* (New York: Carlton & Lanahan, 1844), 26.

68 West, 28.

Gospel of salvation to both masters and slaves."[69] When the votes were taken on Harding's appeal, he lost by a margin of 117 to 56. The ensuing contentiousness of the 1844 General Conference led to the creation of the Methodist Episcopal Church, South, and William Andrew Smith was a prominent figure in the establishment of that proslavery denomination.

In 1846 Smith was elected to the presidency of Randolph-Macon College, Ashland, Virginia. He also taught a course on moral and political philosophy. The president used Francis Wayland's text, *The Elements of Moral Science* (1835), but found Wayland's mildly antislavery perspective objectionable. While Wayland spent relatively few pages on the subject of slavery, William Andrew Smith felt obliged to amend his teaching with a series of thirteen lectures supporting the southern view. In 1856 Smith published these addresses as *Lectures on the Philosophy and Practice of Slavery.*

This comprehensive treatment of the matter is not for the faint of heart. The college president opened his preface by stating that "since the year 1844" he had been called upon to clarify his perspective, and he marshaled all of his resources to do so.[70] The very first lecture demonstrates that Smith either qualified his remarks while speaking before the Methodist Episcopal Church or had become even more strident over the intervening years. Directly out of the gate he posed the question: *"Is the institution of domestic slavery sinful?"*[71] Given the distinction Smith endorsed in 1844, we might expect him to concede that the institution was evil but not necessarily sinful. Instead he answered his question by stating: "The position I propose to maintain in these lectures is, that slavery, *per se*, is right; or that the great abstract principle of slavery is right, because it is a

---

69 West, 28.

70 William A. Smith, *Lectures on the Philosophy and Practice of Slavery, As Exhibited in the Institution of Domestic Slavery in the United States: with the Duties of Masters to Slaves*, Thomas O. Summers, D.D., ed. (Nashville: Stevenson and Evans, 1856), vii. See also the insightful examination of proslavery arguments in the Old South by Alfred L. Brophy: *University, Court, and Slave: Pro-Slavery Thought in Southern Colleges and Courts and the Coming of Civil War* (Oxford: Oxford University Press, 2016).

71 Smith, 11.

fundamental principle of the social state; and that domestic slavery, as an *institution*, is fully justified by the condition and circumstances (essential and relative) of the African race in this country, and therefore equally right."[72] This may strike us as a deontological argument for slavery. There were such things. Claiming that slavery is right, in some basic sense, does not sound like consequentialist logic.

Yet with Smith, reasoning was a rather circuitous endeavor. He maintained that he would not apologize for slavery but would present it in a more positive light. He even criticized fellow Virginian, Thomas Jefferson. Not unlike Thomas Cooper, President Smith regretted the way Jefferson concluded that slavery was sinful, *per se*.[73] Smith did acknowledge that a principle may be right in essence but wrong in practice. However, he claimed that "inequality among men is the will of God; and if his will is the rule of *our rights*, we have no abstract right to equality. It is rather our duty to submit to that inequality of condition which results from the superior intelligence or moral power of others."[74] Smith was especially vexed that the assertion of equality found its way into the Declaration of Independence. This could only have happened because "one of the presiding minds of that great paper had become strongly tinctured with the infidel philosophy of France."[75] Today we labor to make sense of those who celebrated equality and then did not live up to the ideal. On the eve of the Civil War, many resented the idea itself.

William Andrew Smith's first three lectures set the stage for a critical, theoretically dense fourth lecture. Here he took his previous definitions of the "right" and subordinated them to something he called the "essential good." In other words, anything called right is only so because it conforms to the overall good: "The RIGHT then, in itself, is the GOOD. The GOOD is the true generic idea which classifies all the different applications of this

---

72 Smith, 11–12.
73 Smith, 13–16.
74 Smith, 63–64.
75 Smith, 66.

term."[76] After adopting a decidedly teleological or consequentialist frame-work, Smith could then apply his earlier claims to a concern for creating the good.

It is no surprise that the college president found freedom for people of African descent contrary to this good. As Smith argued, "It would not be to them an essential good, but an essential evil, a curse. To confer it on them, either by an act of direct or gradual emancipation, would be eminently productive of injury to the whole country, and utterly ruinous to them."[77] Later he expressed the view this way: "The law of reciprocity and the law of benevolence require that the Africans be continued under an inferior and subordinate government."[78] Such a benevolent fellow as President Smith could not bear to endanger the public welfare and the good of enslaved people!

It is tempting to interpret Smith's views as more nuanced and less venomous than those of Thomas Cooper. This may be so as regarding their respective personalities and styles, but the arguments they make are exceedingly similar. They both denied fundamental notions of equality on the way to asserting white supremacy and maintaining that domestic slav-ery was a public good. We might even wonder if there is much distance between these arguments and the more combative (while less philosophi-cal) claim by John C. Calhoun that slavery was a "positive good." The evidence suggests that they shared much in common.

It is true that these particular, though prominent, professors were not the only teleological thinkers in the Old South. Theoretically, one could invoke some consequentialist reasoning for more just ends. Yet it is strik-ing that the defenders of slavery often relied upon teleological approaches when attempting to justify injustice. Contemporary efforts to dislocate these rationalizations from their context are pointless. It matters not that legendary British consequentialists Jeremy Bentham and John Stuart Mill are remembered as progressive thinkers. Again, the typology of liberal

---

76 Smith, 94.

77 Smith, 182.

78 Smith, 203.

versus conservative, as those concepts are understood today, plays little helpful role in understanding antebellum moral reasoning and its relationship to slavery. The question at hand does not ask whether consequentialism (or more specifically, utilitarianism) inevitably led to the support of slavery. The question, rather, asks whether various kinds of teleological reasoning were employed to defend slavery. They were.

We might even draw a tentative conclusion regarding the trajectory of consequentialist thinking from the American Revolution to the Civil War. In some respects, revolutionary forms of consequentialism, at least that of Samuel Hopkins, offered great promise for creating a just and equitable nation. As time unfolded, we can see where this promise gave way to rationalizations that slavery may be a necessary evil in order to create a greater good. Finally, we can follow the manner in which some mid-nineteenth-century thinkers used consequentialist arguments to defend slavery as an outright good.

These arguments were not simplistic, and they were not put together in haphazard ways. They became finely developed weapons in the arsenal of white supremacy, and they reveal a cautionary tale. Theoretical constructs do not necessitate particular conclusions, but some are more available than others for the rationalizing of preconceived viewpoints. American moral philosophy was never a disembodied discipline. It always lived and breathed among the predetermined agendas of people. Such theory was anything but irrelevant. It played an absolutely critical role as America stumbled toward Civil War.

Three

THE RIGHT FOR ALL?

The Moral Sense in America

Buried in the very same cemetery (at Princeton, New Jersey) where Jonathan Edwards sleeps is a later president of the College of New Jersey (now Princeton University). That later president is John Witherspoon (1723–1794). I had certainly known of him during my undergraduate years and made a visit to his grave, while sleuthing out the resting place of Edwards, but this anecdotal memory reveals a more pervasive dynamic. The tenure of Edwards at Princeton was incredibly and tragically short, but his legacy has managed to birth a multigenerational fan base. Witherspoon, on the other hand, served as president at Princeton from 1768 until his death in 1794. He is not forgotten but is certainly a less-celebrated intellectual. Why so?

Any answer to this question is unavoidably conjectural. For one, Witherspoon, though widely published, is not generally lauded for riveting and original theological analysis. He was the workhorse of a tradition during turbulent times in America. He steadied the institution at Princeton (often called "Nassau Hall," after its original campus building). He broadened the curriculum, and he maintained an amazingly active role in public affairs. John Witherspoon is perhaps best known as a signer of the Declaration of Independence.[1]

---

1 The sweeping and now classic study of philosophy in America by Elizabeth Flower and Murray G. Murphey devotes generous attention to Witherspoon.

Witherspoon was born in Scotland, educated at Edinburgh, and served as a clergyperson of renown among his native land before ever stepping foot in America. He participated in church controversies, defending a direct and (to his mind) more egalitarian ecclesiastical government that made him many friends—and enemies. When the trustees at Princeton needed a new president, various factions lobbied for several candidates. They settled on John Witherspoon, and he crossed the Atlantic to manage affairs at the College of New Jersey.[2]

Witherspoon became the flagbearer of Scottish Common Sense Realism in America. When he arrived in the colonies, Scottish epistemology was not at all the only option available. New England currents tended to entertain the idealism of Bishop George Berkeley, who came to America for a short time and developed a plantation near Newport, Rhode Island. There is also evidence that various forms of deism and skepticism—even materialism—were prevalent. Some of these accounts may have been exaggerated by those hoping to restore more traditional modes of reasoning, but history suggests that the Scottish school, reviled later as a suffocating defense of orthodoxy, was not dominant before the American Revolution.[3]

Therefore, John Witherspoon's arrival from Scotland carried as much symbolic import as it did substantive meaning, which is somewhat ironic— given Witherspoon's practical bent. The new president set about evicting threatening philosophies from Nassau Hall, and he made the developing school of Thomas Reid and others the established framework for teaching and learning. This began with the serviceable metaphysics and epistemology of realism, but it also extended to the study of moral philosophy. John Witherspoon's *Lectures on Moral Philosophy*, delivered to undergraduates long before seeing publication, remains a signature work of the college president. *Lectures* was not published until 1800, and the received

---

Elizabeth Flower and Murray G. Murphey, *A History of Philosophy in America*, Vol. 1 (New York: Capricorn Books, 1977), 203–38.

2   Flower and Murphey, 226–32.

3   Flower and Murphey, 229–32.

text was established by piecing together student-generated manuscripts that were checked against other sources. The first edition appeared in *The Works of the Reverend John Witherspoon*.[4]

In 1912 Varnum Lansing Collins published an edition of the *Lectures* that remains available. Collins explained that he began with the first edition (1800) and compared it to later versions (1810 and 1822). He also checked this text against three transcripts from students of Witherspoon.[5] The document, some 144 pages, is not very innovative. The president followed standard categories and distinctions. His ethical theory was basic, borrowing from many predecessors and perspectives. Yet these lectures did bear Witherspoon's own stamp at critical points.

He employed the familiar faculty psychology of the day—the understanding, the will, and the affections—in a quest for reliable sources of truth.[6] Yet eventually he came to emphasize the moral sense, as might be expected of someone promoting the Scottish school. He described this endowment in a manner very similar to Thomas Reid: "This moral sense is precisely the same thing with what, in scripture and common language, we call conscience. It is the law which our Maker has written upon our hearts, and both intimates and enforces duty, previous to all reasoning."[7] It is, in short, the way we know right from wrong.[8]

Lecture IV turned to the all-important discussion of virtue. What is virtue? What is its foundation? What obligations does it bring? Witherspoon considered a number of possible answers to these questions, and at times he demonstrated an interest in public utility or some definition of

---

4   *The Works of the Reverend John Witherspoon* (Philadelphia: William W. Woodward, 1800).

5   John Witherspoon, *Lectures on Moral Philosophy*, ed. Varnum Lansing Collins (Princeton: Princeton University Press, 1912), xxii–xxiii. See also John Witherspoon, *Lectures on Moral Philosophy*, ed. Jack Scott (Newark: University of Delaware Press, 1982).

6   Witherspoon, 10.

7   Witherspoon, 17–18.

8   Witherspoon, 21.

the good. However, he also expressed concern for making these things the essence of virtue:

> Again, promoting the public or general good seems to be so nearly connected with virtue, that we must necessarily suppose that universal virtue could be of universal utility. Yet there are two excesses to which this has sometimes led.—One the fatalist and necessitarian schemes to which there are so many objections, and the other, the making the general good the ultimate practical rule to every particular person, so that he may violate particular obligations with a view to a more general benefit.[9]

He followed by saying that true virtue certainly promotes the general good but to make the good of the whole our pressing principle of action is "putting ourselves in God's place, and actually superseding the necessity and use of the particular principles of duty which he hath impressed upon the conscience."[10] Ultimately, Witherspoon derived his sense of duty from conscience, not calculations of utility.[11]

This moderately deontological ethic guided the college president's approach to rights. He endorsed a type of social contract and added that: "From this view of society as a voluntary compact, results this principle, that men are originally and by nature equal, and consequently free."[12] It is, therefore, more than a bit befuddling that Witherspoon waffled when considering the issue of slavery. Very soon after his claims regarding equality, he addressed slavery and conceded "that in every state there must be some superior and others inferior, and it is hard to fix the degree of subjection that may fall to the lot of particular persons."[13] He rejected the lawfulness of denying liberty to others through no other rationale than a possession of superior power, and he denounced assertions that slavery was somehow

---

9 Witherspoon, 28–29.

10 Witherspoon, 29.

11 Witherspoon, 30.

12 Witherspoon, 71.

13 Witherspoon, 72–73.

good for those under subjugation. Still, he concluded, "There are many unlawful ways of making slaves, but also some that are lawful."[14] During his day, this may have been considered an admirably narrow acceptance of the institution, but it is acceptance, nonetheless.

Writing in the early twentieth century, Varnum Lansing Collins offered an apology for Witherspoon by noting that in his late years (1790), the college president served in the New Jersey Legislature. There he chaired a committee to consider the abolition of slavery in that state. According to Collins, Witherspoon favored an approach that would pass a law, guaranteeing freedom to those born following its enactment—upon reaching the age of twenty-eight. Yet Collins claimed, President Witherspoon was unshakably convinced that revolutionary ideas of liberty would take root in the new nation, and there would be no more slavery twenty-eight years later.[15] When Witherspoon died on November 15, 1794, his estate included two enslaved people, "valued" at one hundred dollars each.[16]

The inconsistencies of John Witherspoon's theory and practice are perhaps the rule more than they are the exception. We cannot claim to know with certainty why he conceded the acceptable existence of slavery nor why he participated in the injustice himself. We *can* offer an observation regarding his moral philosophy. The president refused to make some clear end—for instance, benevolence or utility—the ultimate measure of right and wrong because such a standard might force a violation of conscience. Witherspoon appears to have suffered from the opposite danger: that of allowing self-interest to work its way through isolated claims of conscience. This was not a rare fault, and many consequentialists saw it as the inevitable product of theories that relied on moral sense. It should be noted that few eighteenth-century consequentialists offered a more just vision for humanity. Witherspoon's school of thought would later nourish

---

14 Witherspoon, 73–74.

15 Witherspoon, 74. See also Varnum Lansing Collins, *President Witherspoon: A Biography*, Vol. 2 (Princeton: Princeton University Press, 1925), 167–68.

16 Collins, 181.

some genuine abolitionists, but this was not the witness of the movement's founder.

Common Sense and the Upper South

In Virginia's Shenandoah Valley, near present-day Lexington, Princeton's next great luminary was born. Archibald Alexander (1772–1851) would become the first professor of Princeton Theological Seminary, a graduate school for Presbyterian clergy just a neighborhood away from Nassau Hall. Yet his early years were spent near the Blue Ridge of Virginia. The time and place of Alexander's upbringing serve as a metaphor for his lifelong and ambivalent relationship with slavery.

The post-revolutionary period contained glimmers of hope for those wanting slavery to end. Even folk in regions that relied on the practice were sometimes uneasy with the juxtaposition of America's founding principles and human bondage. This rather brief moment of introspection was perhaps more pronounced where slavery's existence did not dominate economic life. The Shenandoah Valley was populated by Europeans later than eastern areas. Many inhabitants were of Scotch-Irish or German ancestry who had traveled "up" the Valley (by direction, south) from Pennsylvania. In time, the distinctions would be washed away, but for a while, the Valley was known for small farms, varied crops and livestock, and the fierce independence of residents. The Tidewater to the east was more aristocratic and driven by large tobacco plantations. Slavery did exist in the Shenandoah Valley but not on the scale that prevailed in the Tidewater.[17]

---

17 A study that remains both specific in its focus on Alexander and broad in its treatment of Princeton Theological Seminary is: Lefferts A. Loetscher, *Facing the Enlightenment and Pietism: Archibald Alexander and the Founding of Princeton Theological Seminary* (Westport, Connecticut: Greenwood Press, 1983), especially 3–14. See also James H. Moorhead's bicentennial study of Princeton Theological Seminary: James H. Moorhead, *Princeton Seminary in American Religion and Culture* (Grand Rapids, Michigan: William B. Eerdmans Publishing Company, 2012).

Into this culture came Archibald Alexander on April 17, 1772. During his teens he studied at Liberty Hall, a predecessor academy of today's Washington and Lee University, and his mentor was Rev. William Graham, a 1773 graduate of the College of New Jersey (Princeton). At one point, family members encouraged Alexander to finish his studies in Princeton, but he received plenty of Princeton-like pedagogy from Graham, who passed along the perspective of John Witherspoon. Archibald Alexander did not merely parrot Witherspoon throughout his life and teaching, but there was much of Witherspoon among his early influences.[18]

Alexander was ordained in 1794 and served churches in Virginia. At least one of these congregations "owned" enslaved people both before and after Alexander's pastorate—and presumably during that time, as well.[19] The young pastor served as the third president of Hampden-Sydney College before moving to Philadelphia, where he was installed at the Third Presbyterian Church in 1807. The move to Philadelphia meant that the Alexander family had to confront the legality of slavery. Alexander's wife, Janetta, "owned" a woman who had been bound to her for several years. The laws of Pennsylvania placed limits on the institution of slavery, even though the process of abolition was gradual at the time.[20]

Letters, proposals, and some intrigue suggesting the need for an independent Presbyterian graduate seminary date from at least 1805. By 1812 the various ideas coalesced in a plan that received support from the church's General Assembly. Princeton, New Jersey, would be the location of a new seminary, devoted to the education of clergy. While not directly linked to the governance structure of the town's college, the two institutions shared similar cultures and even some overlap of leadership.

---

18 Loetscher, *Facing the Enlightenment and Pietism: Archibald Alexander and the Founding of Princeton Theological Seminary*, 27–40.

19 Loetscher, 53.

20 Moorhead, *Princeton Seminary in American Religion and Culture*, 42.

Archibald Alexander was selected to serve as the first professor at Princeton Theological Seminary.[21]

Alexander met his task with determination, though the initial student community was exceedingly small. One of his earliest lectures addressed the "Nature and Evidence of Truth." If there was any question regarding the epistemology that would ground the new seminary, such inquiry was put to rest with this lecture. Archibald Alexander made it abundantly clear that his students would be taught from the context of Scottish Common Sense.[22]

This primary orientation was then applied to a host of studies, including moral philosophy. Alexander's text on moral philosophy was not issued until the year following his death, in 1852, but the formal release made public a series of lectures students had received for several decades. The preface to this posthumous work notes that the professor was pained by the extent to which William Paley's ethic ruled the day.[23] He accepted the challenge of offering an alternative, and he did so in a manner reminiscent of John Witherspoon.

The very first page of his text claimed that all people possess a power of "discerning a difference between actions, as to their moral quality. The judgment thus formed is immediate, and has no relation to the usefulness or injuriousness to human happiness, of the objects contemplated."[24] In other words, Alexander saw the idea of moral good or virtue as entirely distinct from that of utility.[25] This line of reasoning made him a deontologist who sought to overcome some perceived assault on proper ethics by Paley's utilitarianism, but several joined together in this effort. Alexander's overall approach was not unique.

---

21 Loetscher, *Facing the Enlightenment and Pietism: Archibald Alexander and the Founding of Princeton Theological Seminary,* 109–38.

22 See Mark. A. Noll, ed., *The Princeton Theology: 1812–1921* (Grand Rapids, Michigan: Baker Book House, 1983), 61–71.

23 Archibald Alexander, *Outlines of Moral Science* (New York: Charles Scribner, 1852), 15.

24 Alexander, 19.

25 Alexander, 29.

Moreover, by the early nineteenth century, Scottish Common Sense philosophy was sufficiently established in America to make its re-articulation nothing new. Archibald Alexander relied on some form of moral sense or conscience to determine right and wrong, and one may be pardoned for concluding that his ethic was little more than an extension of familiar concepts. Yet Alexander's particular treatment included somewhat unusual distinctions and combinations. There are points where his thinking is refreshingly detailed, even as there are points where it seems almost contradictory.

For instance, while he suggested that conscience acted in a direct way, he did not claim that it was simple and unrelated to other powers. He viewed it as closely allied with judgment and moral feeling: "The conclusion, therefore is that conscience is not a distinct faculty from reason, so far as it consists in a judgment of the quality of moral acts. Reason or understanding is the genus; the judgments of conscience are the species."[26] There is a certain insight to this approach, but it also opens more questions.

Does this sort of complexity mean that conscience is somehow in need of corresponding reflection or even comparison to an innate moral law? Alexander resisted the latter implication by asserting that the operations of the mind are always from particulars to generals—that is, inductive—and not determined by a pre-established universal law.[27] On the whole, he seemed to be aware of the problems involved in his more complicated treatment of the moral sense, but we might wonder if he ever really managed to get the ideas sorted out completely.

Of particular interest is Alexander's analysis of whether or not conscience can ever be wrong. To say that it could might imply that his whole epistemology stood on insecure foundations, but he did not see things this way. Instead he suggested that a perfectly competent moral sense or conscience could be clouded by prejudice. This did not excuse wrong behavior, nor did it mean that conscience, in itself, is unreliable. He used the language of illumination to argue that truths or the method of knowing

26 Alexander, 43.
27 Alexander, 75.

them do not change. Rather, ignorance, error, or prejudice may prevent us from seeing truth in the proper light.[28]

Contemporary readers may find an honesty, if not clarity, in Archibald Alexander's moral philosophy. There is something disarming and earnest about admitting that "prejudice" may make moral judgments more challenging than many Scottish philosophers claimed. However, positing the danger of prejudice as a theoretical problem is one thing. Identifying the ways this problem enters into one's own moral conclusions is something else entirely.

We might even suggest that Archibald Alexander's interaction with slavery illustrates the obstacles that accompany theories of conscience. Alexander's text on moral philosophy did not give extended treatment to the social issues of his day, but other sources show him grappling with serious matters, including slavery. One such document is a letter he wrote in response to correspondence from Rev. William S. Plumer (1802–1880). Plumer attended Washington College in Lexington, Virginia (now Washington and Lee), then Princeton Seminary. By 1829 he was serving the same Briery, Virginia, church where Alexander had been pastor years before. The parallels between professor and former student are striking, and Plumer would go on to hold prominent leadership positions among southern Presbyterianism. In June of 1830 Archibald Alexander offered his protégé advice concerning the relationship between ministry and slavery.[29]

It appears that young William Plumer was concerned with how he should approach the ministry in a culture that affirmed slavery. Given Plumer's earlier education in this same region, we have little to indicate that he disapproved of bondage. In fact, Alexander's letter implies that Plumer "owned" other people. Still, what was the pastor's responsibility in such a society? Professor Alexander advised Plumer to remain in his present context and to "endeavour by all lawful means to extend the blessing

---

28 Alexander, 64–72, 188.

29 Henry Alexander White, *Southern Presbyterian Leaders* (New York: The Neale Publishing Company, 1911), 286–92.

of salvation to that degraded people."[30] Alexander never challenged the institution. He reasoned that Plumer would discharge his duties best by keeping the enslaved in his "possession" and by "instructing them in the Christian religion."[31]

Alexander admitted that it was difficult to offer conclusive judgment, since he was so far removed from Plumer's situation, but we might suggest that any judgment offered by Alexander was very much informed by his upbringing in the same locale.[32] Perhaps here was an instance of "conscience" being distorted by ignorance, error—or at least, prejudice. This does not mean that right and wrong are unavoidably relative, but we should acknowledge the way Archibald Alexander's compromising approach to slavery was informed (or deformed) by his background.

The Antislavery Turn: Francis Wayland

Over two decades ago, by sweet accident, I stepped into a Midwestern book shop and found a first-edition copy of Francis Wayland's legendary text, *The Elements of Moral Science* (1835). The book was in poor condition, but I did not mind. This text marked a departure in American moral philosophy, not so much for its originality but for the fact that it popularized a deontological ethic precisely at the time when most colleges were becoming tired of William Paley. Wayland's book also tackled the issue of slavery and argued against it, albeit in a rather modest manner. One might see in the contrast between Paley's utilitarianism and Wayland's deontological theory (along with Wayland's indictment of slavery) proof that the former approach was more available to defenders of bondage, while the latter was linked to freedom. As things turned out in America, there is much truth to this conclusion, but simply comparing Paley and Wayland to prove the point is disingenuous. The story is more complex.

---

30 This letter and others are published in a biography of Archibald Alexander written by his son, James W. Alexander, in 1854. See James W. Alexander, *The Life of Archibald Alexander, D. D.* (New York: Charles Scribner, 1854), 522.

31 Alexander, 522.

32 Alexander, 521–22.

After all, John Witherspoon and Archibald Alexander both embraced a deontological conscience theory and participated in slavery, while Paley offered a mild rebuke of the institution. Wayland's text marked a departure as much within the movement of deontological thinkers as it did among the wider teaching of moral philosophy. Moreover, American college professors appreciated Wayland's book for less theoretical reasons. Witherspoon's ethic had been pieced together and published at the turn of the nineteenth century, but it never saw the use in various colleges enjoyed by Wayland's text. Alexander's lectures were standard at Princeton Seminary, but they were not published until 1852. Francis Wayland released his book exactly at a point when those who agreed with him and those who did not could enjoy the fact that one of their own had dethroned British dominance (Paley). America now hailed a popular and indigenous teaching resource on moral philosophy. It is generally claimed that Francis Wayland's book sold more than 100,000 copies, in a day when that number was near astronomical.[33]

The copy of Wayland's moral philosophy that fell into my possession is significant for many reasons. First, the bookplate reads, "Library of the Theological Seminary, Princeton, N.J.," and second, it contains some provocative marginalia on the pages that address slavery. I stumbled onto a first edition copy of Wayland's book that was originally in the library of Princeton Theological Seminary (most probably during the Alexander years)—a copy that was contested by readers, perhaps members of the Princeton community.

Francis Wayland (1796–1865) was born in New York City. He was the son of a leather merchant and was graduated from Union College in 1813. He studied medicine for a while but felt called to the Baptist ministry. He spent a relatively short time at Andover Seminary before serving as pastor in Boston. In 1827 he was called to the presidency of Brown University, where he served until 1855. Wayland was a person of energy and tact (an unusual combination for the time). He was an educational reformer, and he

---

33 Meyer, *The Instructed Conscience*, 13–14.

was not afraid to take progressive stands on several social issues, though he was known as someone who rarely attacked the person of his opponents. Wayland was also a moderate Calvinist, appreciating the overall teachings of that tradition while putting more emphasis on human agency.[34]

A close reading of *The Elements of Moral Science* is revealing. When one peels back the interpretive layers that have developed among scholars over more than 180 years, one finds an intriguing argument. The preface expressed Wayland's dissatisfaction with Paley and plainly acknowledged a debt to Bishop Joseph Butler and his form of conscience theory.[35] Early on, the president defined moral behavior as "the voluntary action of an intelligent agent, who is capable of distinguishing between right and wrong, or of distinguishing what he ought, from what he ought not to do."[36] The task then became determining *how* an agent can distinguish between right and wrong with some confidence.

For a good portion of his text, Wayland followed the established script of conscience theorists: "It seems, then, from what has been remarked, that we are all endowed with conscience, or a faculty for discerning a moral quality in human actions, impelling us towards right, and dissuading us from wrong; and that the dictates of this faculty, are felt and known to be, of supreme authority."[37] Such a comprehensive statement is followed, however, by a chapter bearing the title: "Imperfections of Conscience; Necessity of Some Additional Moral Light."[38] This acknowledgment appears similar to the concern expressed by Alexander (and others) that things are not always as clear as claimed. Yet perhaps unlike Alexander, Wayland thought he could define the necessary supplement. He argued that, "the sources of moral light, irrespective of conscience" are twofold: the precepts

---

34 Meyer, 13–14.
35 Francis Wayland, *The Elements of Moral Science* (New York: Cooke and Co., 1835), ix–ii.
36 Wayland, 9.
37 Wayland, 73.
38 Wayland, 107–14.

of natural religion and the precepts and motives of the sacred Scriptures.[39] The first relied on the teachings of nature, the second, revelation.

Whether Wayland offered a plausible solution to the problems of conscience may be disputed, but with this foundation he tackled "practical ethics" or the general responsibilities of people among society. In a section devoted to duties we owe one another, Wayland argued: "The relation in which men stand to each other, is essentially the relation of equality."[40] Interestingly, he turned a distinction often employed by proslavery writers upon its head. Wayland granted that there was an inequality of "condition" (various talents, physical strength, station in society, etc.) but that this did not mean there was an inequality of "right." Southern writers advancing notions of racial superiority often invoked the inequality of condition to bolster their claims that some justifiably possess more rights than others. Wayland was not buying this tactic. He believed the opposite to be the case. Rights were based upon nature and divine authority. To make rights dependent upon existing condition was to make them subject to arbitrary advantage—advantage that often changed according to the vicissitudes of human power.[41]

This discussion led to an analysis of personal liberty and the issue of slavery. Francis Wayland's examination of slavery was not exhaustive, but it was fairly clear. Early in his remarks about the matter, he asserted that, "Slavery, thus, violates the personal liberty of man as a physical, intellectual, and moral being."[42] He continued by stating that slavery gives the master a right to control the labor of the enslaved, not for the happiness of those in bonds but for the sake of the master's happiness. The marginal notation in the copy of Wayland's text previously mentioned reads: "This is an assumption."[43] On the next page the same hand has written: "This

---

39 Wayland, 112.
40 Wayland, 201.
41 Wayland, 201–9.
42 Wayland, 220.
43 Wayland, 220.

argument is illogical & inconclusive."[44] If these notations were scribbled at Princeton, it would appear that some in the community had a hard time with Wayland's rather modest antislavery stance.

Later, Francis Wayland would debate slavery with Beaufort, South Carolina, pastor Richard Fuller. The two exchanged letters among the *Christian Reflector*, and the robust, yet relatively civil, discourse was published in book form as *Domestic Slavery Considered as a Scriptural Institution* (1845).[45] Wayland attempted to remain in relationship with Christian representatives of the South, and northern activists could not really consider him an abolitionist. Yet as the 1840s and 1850s unfolded, he found himself less able to reach across sectional lines. By the time the Civil War erupted, Francis Wayland was a full-throated advocate for freedom. Matthew S. Hill has argued that, while Wayland was pushed and pulled by events, his witness was guided by ideas present in his early writing.[46] Francis Wayland's story reminds us that iconic texts of moral philosophy do not appear without context and cease to have meaning when the world changes. They live on as implicit principles lead to timely practice.

Quakers and Conscience

The Religious Society of Friends may be one of the most lauded and least understood movements in Christian history. Regardless of political affiliation, many cannot help but respect the Quaker emphasis on serving others, nonviolence, and egalitarianism. Yet the sheer diversity of Quaker communities around the globe and the assumptions of outside admirers combine to make appropriate understanding a challenge. In America, the Friends are often lumped together as one undifferentiated body, when there are, in fact, several expressions of the tradition. This is a shame. Such objectification only serves to make a complicated and compelling

---

44 Wayland, 221.

45 Richard Fuller and Francis Wayland, *Domestic Slavery Considered as a Scriptural Institution* (New York: Lewis Colby, 1845).

46 Matthew S. Hill, "God and Slavery in America: Francis Wayland and the Evangelical Conscience" (PhD diss., Georgia State University, 2008).

tradition the stuff of one-dimensional heroes. The Religious Society of Friends deserves better, even if an honest examination of the Quaker experience reveals the same flaws and gifts shared by most movements.

It might seem an extension of the stereotypes to focus on the colonial leadership of William Penn, but by examining his work we find that he was not only a seminal leader, he was also a shaper of Quaker theology. Penn (1644–1718) was born in England and lived a life of both great privilege and repudiation of that privilege. He wrote controversial religious tracts that landed him in the Tower of London (1668) when these publications were judged threats to Anglican authority. Penn was promised freedom if he would recant his printed convictions. Instead he stuck to his principles and wrote, among other things, the classic text, *No Cross, No Crown*. Here he combined the Quaker emphasis on conscience with the light of Christ. In the preface to one edition of this work, Penn addressed those who desired truth and the way of discipleship: "I exhort and invite thee to embrace the reproofs and convictions of Christ's light and spirit in thine own conscience, and bear the judgment, who hast wrought the sin."[47] Penn attributed the corruption of Christianity in his day to the neglect of this light and conscience. He stated that established religious powers "didst decline to audit accounts, in thy own conscience, with Christ thy light, the great bishop of thy soul."[48] Such bold communication won him many enemies but also the begrudging respect of some opponents.

Our memory of Penn as a practical person devoted to community development and religious freedom should not overshadow the specific theological and philosophical emphases that guided him. Later Quakers added their own variations on the twin themes of light and conscience. One such person was nineteenth-century English writer Caroline Emelia Stephen (1834–1909). Through several reflective and devotional publications

---

47 William Penn, *No Cross, No Crown: A Discourse Shewing the Nature and Discipline of the Holy Cross of Christ; and that the Denial of Self, and Daily Bearing of Christ's Cross, is the Alone Way to the Rest and Kingdom of God* (Philadelphia: T. K. & P. G. Collins, 1853), 4.

48 Penn, 28–29.

Stephen made clear that, among the diversity of the Religious Society of Friends, some principles remained. In her book, *Quaker Strongholds* (1890), she wrote, "The one corner-stone of belief upon which the Society of Friends is built is the conviction that God does indeed communicate with each one of the spirits."[49] Later in this text she elaborated: "Our testimonies are, in fact, to a degree which is, I think, hardly understood outside the Society, the result of individual and spontaneous obedience to the bidding of individual conscience, and to the guiding of the Divine light shining in each heart, rather than of conformity to rules enforced or even precisely laid down by any human authority."[50] This latter remark touches on the intriguing tension between conscience theories and rules-based frameworks.

Today the legacy of light and conscience lives on, especially in that iteration of the Friends community known as the "Conservative Quakers of America." One statement puts the relationship between the two emphases this way: "It is also the Light that teaches us the difference between right and wrong, truth and falseness, good and evil. It guides our conscience, but it is not the conscience itself. Our conscience is our own mental organ which perceives the Light from God, but in different individuals the conscience might be poorly developed or even mistaken."[51] Though from a dramatically different theological context, there is almost something akin to Archibald Alexander's reservations about the clarity of conscience here.

The Religious Society of Friends is often remembered as a leader in the growing colonial consciousness against slavery. There is much evidence for this claim and for the general narrative of Quakers as antislavery people. Yet this is not the whole story. The early movement in America was actually divided over the issue, and some members of the Friends lived

---

49 Caroline Emelia Stephen, *Quaker Strongholds* (London: Kegan Paul, Trench, Trubner & Co., Lt., 1890), 20.

50 Stephen, 126.

51 Conservative Quakers of America, accessed July 24, 2017, www.quaker.us /inwardlight.html.

privileged lives that benefited from slavery.[52] Perhaps especially disturbing is the participation of William Penn and his family in the institution.[53]

Later Quakers, such as John Woolman in New Jersey (1720–1772) and others, helped turn the tide among the tradition, and by the nineteenth century many within the Religious Society of Friends were admirably out front of the dominant culture. Throughout the Ohio Valley and Old Northwest (and in the East) a network developed among those who assisted seekers of freedom on the Underground Railroad. Levi and Catharine Coffin became legends within the movement, and Levi (1798–1877) wrote an autobiography. Coffin was born in North Carolina but moved to eastern Indiana and then to Cincinnati. His book not only recalled activity in the abolitionist movement; it also revealed the motivation and leading principles of his family's witness. Not surprisingly, the Quaker emphasis on conscience played a central role in his more practical commitments.

When explaining his antislavery activities, Coffin noted the resistance he and others received from many quarters. As he saw things: "We asked only liberty of conscience—freedom to act according to one's conscientious convictions."[54] This same reasoning applied to Coffin's efforts at creating a "free labor" movement (today known as the "Fair Trade" movement). He resolved "as a matter of conscience" to abstain from products generated by slavery and even ordered his business practices to support free labor.[55] Levi Coffin was hardly a philosopher of the moral sense or conscience, but it mattered to him greatly.

---

52 This story is told in Jean R. Soderlund, *Quakers and Slavery: A Divided Spirit* (Princeton, New Jersey: Princeton University Press, 1985).

53 See Gary B. Nash and Jean R. Soderlund, *Freedom by Degrees: Emancipation in Pennsylvania and Its Aftermath* (Oxford: Oxford University Press, 1991), 12.

54 Levi Coffin, *Reminiscences of Levi Coffin, The Reputed President of the Underground Railroad; Being a Brief History of the Labors of a Lifetime in Behalf of the Slave, with the Stories of Numerous Fugitives, Who Gained their Freedom through His Instrumentality, and Many Other Incidents,* 2nd ed., with Appendix (Cincinnati: Robert Clarke & Co., 1880), 230.

55 Coffin, 268–69.

The same could be said for one of Coffin's fellow conspirators on the Underground Railroad. Laura Haviland (1808–1898) was born in Leeds County, part of what is now eastern Ontario. She was grounded in the Society of Friends but also attended meetings of the Methodists. The contrast in styles between these two traditions did not please her parents, but later, in 1841, Haviland and much of her family joined the emerging abolitionist sect of Wesleyan Methodists in Michigan. Quaker by ancestry and Wesleyan by affiliation, Haviland became a treasured host among Michigan's Underground Railroad. She was buried in a Quaker graveyard near Adrian, Michigan.[56] Throughout her life she sprinkled her writing and activism with mentions of conscience, as well as more Wesleyan-sounding references to unlimited atonement. Once, when summoned to the Coffin home in Cincinnati as part of a plan to free someone held in bondage, Haviland resolved to travel on the Sabbath. Perhaps she should wait, but her conclusion was swift: "It was lawful on the Sabbath to lift a sheep out of the ditch in the days of Moses, and is not a man better than a sheep?" The language of her telling invoked the dictates of conscience over rules.[57]

Perhaps one of the deepest writers to combine the Quaker appreciation for conscience and the abolitionist cause was Laura Haviland's Michigan "neighbor," Elizabeth Margaret Chandler. Chandler (already mentioned in the first chapter) lived a few miles from the Haviland home and died of disease before her twenty-seventh birthday. She and Haviland formed one of the region's earliest antislavery societies, and Chandler's published poems and brief essays offer insight into her moral/philosophical turn of mind.[58]

---

56 The primary source for biographical information about Haviland is her text: *A Woman's Life-Work: Labors and Experiences of Laura S. Haviland* (Chicago: C. V. Waite & Company, Publishers, 1887).

57 Haviland, 109.

58 A fine introduction to Chandler is Marcia J. Heringa Mason's book, *Remember the Distance that Divides Us: The Family Letters of Philadelphia Quaker Abolitionist and Michigan Pioneer Elizabeth Margaret Chandler, 1830–1842* (East Lansing, Michigan: Michigan State University Press, 2004).

Among Elizabeth Chandler's essays is a piece titled, "Right and Wrong." She opens by remarking how most will agree that one wrong does not excuse another—unless the latter is perpetrated by us. She scorned such self-interested logic: "If we had no conscience; if the laws of God were neither written upon our hearts, nor within the volume of truth, this plea might justly be available."[59] However, it is her reflection titled, "The Voice of Conscience," that links our moral faculties directly to the issue of slavery:

> It is frequently urged as a plea for indifference and inaction with regard to Emancipation, that the mind has never been particularly impressed with the subject, and that the conscience has always remained at rest concerning it. But this we do not conceive to be by any means a valid argument, unless we have diligently called upon, and carefully attended to the suggestions of the mental counsellor. Conscience does not always give her advice unasked; we sometimes walk blindly in a wrong path; but, though we may perhaps be held guiltless, so long as we remain unconsciously slumbering, yet, if we obstinately turn away from the hand that would awaken us, and refuse to open our eyes that we may discover whether light or darkness is around us, surely, we are not less culpable than if we knowingly persisted in error.[60]

This was from a Quaker writer who acknowledged the challenges of relying on conscience, while not excusing immoral behavior. Others would invoke the terminology of conscience to fight slavery, but they would also make some kind of moral law more explicit and universally available to advocates for justice.

---

59 Chandler, *The Poetical Works of Elizabeth Margaret Chandler: Essays Philanthropic and Moral*, 34.
60 Chandler, 107–8.

Transcendentalism

One year following the uprising in Detroit and in my hometown of Benton Harbor, Michigan, Edward H. Madden (a philosopher) wrote an incisive treatment of nineteenth-century moral philosophy and civil disobedience. His text, *Civil Disobedience and Moral Law in Nineteenth-Century American Philosophy*, was published in 1968, the year Martin Luther King Jr. was murdered. Madden addressed a number of thinkers, but his trenchant (if brief) exploration of Transcendentalism is noteworthy. He stated that, "The whole burden of transcendentalism, in a way, is antiutilitarian."[61] This did not mean that those identified with Transcendentalism offered rigorous philosophical critiques of utility, but the movement's spirit was contrary to the cost/benefit analysis of consequentialism.

The entirety of Transcendentalism is far beyond the scope of our consideration here. The movement still raises questions of categorization. Was it primarily literary? Philosophical? Cultural (with echoes of Boston-area privilege)? Not only were there so many voices speaking under the banner of Transcendentalism; the school exuded a kind of pride in defying definition. Yet it did generate concrete expression.

Most scholars note the establishment of a literary circle in 1836 as the closest thing to a founding of Transcendentalism. Reaction to the staid intellectual habits among Unitarian Harvard, as well as the empirical philosophies that dominated British writers, moved a handful of seekers to explore thought emanating from Germany. For the most part, this fascination with German "transcendental" currents was absorbed in a secondhand manner—from the work of Samuel Taylor Coleridge and a few Scottish writers sympathetic to German trends. Nevertheless, American Transcendentalism was something new, in concept if not always in language.[62]

---

61 Edward H. Madden, *Civil Disobedience and Moral Law in Nineteenth-Century American Philosophy* (Seattle and London: University of Washington Press, 1968), 98.

62 See especially Philip F. Gura, *American Transcendentalism: A History* (New York: Hill and Wang, 2007), 69–97.

Ralph Waldo Emerson (1803–1882) captured the vibe and even a few precise philosophical commitments of the movement. His lecture, "The Transcendentalist," is a case in point. First given in 1842, this address has received much scrutiny ever after. In 1949 it was published within a compact anthology given the title: *The Transcendentalist Revolt against Materialism*. The materialism named here is not simply commercialism. It is the formal philosophy we have already encountered that reduces all of life to the interaction of material reality and our experience of this mundane process. The title of this mid-twentieth-century treatment hits the nail on the head. Emerson's famed essay proclaims:

> What is popularly called Transcendentalism among us, is Idealism; Idealism as it appears in 1842. As thinkers, mankind have ever divided into two sects, Materialists and Idealists; the first class founding on experience, the second on consciousness; the first class beginning to think from the data of the senses, the second class perceive that the senses are not final, and say, the senses give us representations of things, but what are the things themselves, they cannot tell.[63]

It should come as no surprise that Immanuel Kant was lurking behind this American movement. Emerson said so outright when he acknowledged that "the Idealism of the present day acquired the name of Transcendental from the use of that term by Immanuel Kant, of Konigsberg."[64] This general adaptation of Kantian metaphysics invites us to consider whether Emerson or any other Transcendentalist invoked Kant's moral philosophy. To an extent, they did.

Samuel Taylor Coleridge offered a paraphrase of the Categorical Imperative as the nineteenth century opened: "So act that thou mayest be able, without involving any contradiction, to will that

---

63 Emerson's essay is found on pages 18–28 of this text. See *The Transcendentalist Revolt against Materialism*, ed. George F. Whicher (Boston: D. C. Heath and Company, 1949), 18.

64 Whicher, 21.

the Maxim of thy Conduct should be the Law of all intelligent Beings."[65] We should be careful about linking this redaction of the Imperative with Emerson's thought, but Emerson did repeat Kant's Imperative approvingly in his piece on "Civilization": "Hear the definition which Kant gives of moral conduct. 'Act always so, that the immediate motive of thy will may become a universal rule for all intelligent beings.' "[66] Overall, however, Emerson's idiosyncratic habits and opinions were little interested in the finer points of Kant's ponderous theory.[67] The Konigsberg seer was more inspiration than explication for Ralph Waldo Emerson.

Theodore Parker (1810–1860) made lucid that which Emerson left poetically vague. A fellow Boston-area clergyperson who embraced Transcendentalist thinking, Parker pursued the movement's principles straight into the fight against slavery. Sometime near 1850 (no one is quite sure) he gave an address titled "Transcendentalism." The lecture was published following his death, in 1876, and there is much of Emerson's metaphysical dichotomy throughout the text. Yet, Parker took the perspectives of Idealism and Materialism and applied them to particular ethical positions, even political movements.

The Idealists were, as may be expected, the "transcendental" school, and the Materialists were the "sensational" school. Parker began by dissecting the sensationalists. Their metaphysics concluded that "all is matter."[68] Perhaps most interesting is Parker's take on the political implications of this sensationalist/materialist view.

---

65 Samuel Taylor Coleridge, *The Friend; A Series of Essays* (London: Gale and Curtis, 1812), 137.

66 "Civilization," *The Collected Works of Ralph Waldo Emerson*, Vol. 7, ed. Ronald A. Bosco and Douglas Emory Wilson (Cambridge: The Belknap Press of Harvard University Press, 2007), 13. See also Vol. 10, 398.

67 This point is made in Lawrence Buell, *Emerson* (Cambridge: The Belknap Press of Harvard University Press, 2003), 211.

68 Theodore Parker, *The World of Matter and The Spirit of Man: Latest Discourses of Religion*, ed. George Willis Cooke (Boston: American Unitarian Association, 1907), 10.

As he analyzed the perspective: "Sensationalism knows nothing of absolute right, absolute justice; only of historical right, historical justice."[69] Parker linked this to the notion that might makes right and later explained in more detail: "For the majority has power of its own right, for its own behoof; not in trust, and for the good of all and each! The aim of sensational politics is the greatest good of the greatest number; this may be obtained by sacrificing the greatest good of the lesser number."[70] He even associated this metaphysical lens with the political ideology of John C. Calhoun: "There is no right, says Mr. Calhoun, but might; the white man has that, so the black man is his political prey."[71] At this point the editor of Parker's text mentions South Carolina's Thomas Cooper and the moral relativism embraced by many white supremacists.[72]

Theodore Parker excelled at typological thinking—placing practical behaviors within the context of their theoretical assumptions. However, he did confront the issue of slavery in plain and forceful ways. This was the case when he released *A Letter to the People of the United States Touching the Matter of Slavery* (1848). The "letter" turned out to be 120 pages long and featured bracing observations. He insisted that slavery began and must be sustained by violence. Sounding rather Kantian, at least in expression, he concluded: "Regarding the slave as a thing, 'an instrument of husbandry,' the master gives him the least, and takes the most that is possible."[73] Parker was not a tepid abolitionist.

In the spring of 1854 a man named Anthony Burns was arrested in Boston and held as a fugitive. A Virginia plantation owner claimed to "own" Burns. Many in Boston rallied to support the arrested man, and Theodore Parker was one of the orators leading the resistance. After a

---

69 Parker, 10.

70 Parker, 12.

71 Parker, 13–14.

72 Parker, 400.

73 Theodore Parker, *A Letter to the People of the United States Touching the Matter of Slavery* (Boston: James Munroe and Company, 1848), 29.

clash, the court delivered Burns to the Virginian.[74] On June 18, 1854, Theodore Parker gave a sermon on "The Law of God and the Statutes of Men." This address came to be one of many that articulated support for a "higher law." Parker opened his preaching by deferring to conscience when considering matters of right and wrong, but he soon began to compare what he called the "statutes" or positive laws of society and the "law" of God.

In short, he would not concede that the "fugitive slave" provisions within the Compromise of 1850 were law. He rested his case on the loyalty people owe divine law, whether that is or is not expressed in statutory form: "Now then, as it is a moral duty to obey a just statute because it is just, so it is a moral duty to disobey any statute which is unjust."[75] Near the end of his sermon he proclaimed: "Without a reverence for the Higher Law of God every thing will be ruled by interest or violence."[76] Parker had witnessed this rule of raw power when Anthony Burns was rendered over to someone who claimed him as property.

Throughout the years, observers have almost assumed that the notion of a "higher law" was exclusive to Boston. This was not the case. Transcendentalism, with its diffuse and sometimes intentionally ill-defined Kantian sympathies, contributed much to higher law thinking. Yet there were evangelical Christians in the heartland (as well as in New England) who advanced a commitment to the higher law.

Evangelicals and the Higher Law

Ask any historian about the higher law tradition and most will immediately reference a response to the "fugitive slave" obligations included in the Compromise of 1850. This makes sense, given that 1850 marked the beginning of much organized civil disobedience to the new statute. However, the articulation of a higher law doctrine can be found among

---

74 Philip F. Gura, *American Transcendentalism: A History*, 252–53.

75 Theodore Parker, *Additional Speeches, Addresses, and Occasional Sermons*, Vol. II (New York: D. Appleton and Company, 1864), 198.

76 Parker, 210–11.

the writings of some well before that fateful year. In fact, the tradition has very, very deep roots.[77]

Within American evangelicalism Luther Lee (1800–1889) was one prophetic soul who brought the emphasis forward. Lee was born in Schoharie, New York, and grew up among poverty. His mother, a devoted Methodist, died when Lee was thirteen, and he was pretty well on his own from that point forward. He married a school teacher, Mary Miller, in 1825, and she is often credited with guiding his belated education. Lee preached throughout various appointments in New York State and was won to the abolitionist cause in 1837. When the Wesleyan Methodist Connection split from the Methodist Episcopal Church over slavery in 1843, Lee was a principal leader of the new movement. His aggressive and methodical style earned him the nickname "Logical Lee." In 1856 Luther Lee published a text on systematic theology that would guide the Wesleyan Methodists for some years.[78]

A second-edition copy of Lee's *Elements*, published in 1859 and now in my possession, has the following verse scribbled in pencil on the inside, front cover:

> This is the work of Luther Lee
> His logic all is plain to me
> His chapters all refreshment give
> To such as truly seek to live
> No darkness here to dim the sight
> But all is plain in reason's light
> The traveler may safely trust
> That wisdom's ways are always blest
>
> C. S.

---

77 See the study by George Edward Carter, "The Use of the Doctrine of Higher Law in the American Anti-Slavery Crusade, 1830–1860" (PhD diss., University of Oregon, 1970).

78 Luther Lee, *Five Sermons and a Tract*, ed. Donald W. Dayton (Chicago: Holrad House, 1975), 9–10.

As with Francis Wayland, once more we observe the way marginalia and other forms of reader response tell us much about a text's reception. We might especially note the language focusing on "logic" and "reason."[79]

Various metaphysical perspectives certainly gravitated toward specific regions and cultures (Idealism in New England, Scottish Common Sense in the Middle States, and Materialism in parts of the South). There were also regional expressions of theological tradition. New York State (as distinguished from New England) hosted many Protestant evangelicals—Trinitarian advocates—who embraced the abolitionist message. Such was the context for Luther Lee's ministry.

In the 1840s Lee followed the story of Charles Turner Torrey. A Congregationalist pastor, Torrey was arrested in Baltimore for aiding the escape of enslaved people. He was sentenced to six years of hard labor but died in 1846 from tuberculosis, while imprisoned. The judicial abuse of Torrey prompted many antislavery voices to cry out. Luther Lee was among them. That year he preached a landmark sermon given the title, "The Supremacy of the Divine Law."

Unlike most Transcendentalists, Lee wove the biblical narrative through his address. Yet he still invoked the revolutionary principles of America's founding. When he came to the task of defining the "divine law," he stated: "The design of divine law is to reveal or make known to man what is right; the design of human law is to secure what is already known to be right."[80] In short, Lee endorsed the fundamental conviction that statutes are to reflect divine law; they do not create ultimate law. With this framework he answered those who accused Charles Torrey of being rash or lacking discretion: "In a word, his rashness and indiscretion were the result of the standard of virtue which he had adopted, which *dares to do right*!"[81] Luther Lee was not exactly a philosopher of the deontological

---

79 Luther Lee, *Elements of Theology, or an Exposition of the Divine Origin, Doctrines, Morals and Institutions of Christianity*, 2nd ed. (Syracuse, New York: Samuel Lee, 1859).

80 Lee, *Five Sermons and a Tract*, 52.

81 Lee, 54.

tradition, but as a theologian, writer, and activist he certainly employed the principle of "right" to attack slavery.

Lee participated in the Underground Railroad over the course of many years, especially while a pastor in Syracuse, New York. Nearby was another Methodist writer and newspaper editor who promoted the notion of a higher law. William Hosmer (1810–1889) called Auburn, New York, his home and wrote in 1852 a book with the title *The Higher Law, in its Relations to Civil Government: with Particular Reference to Slavery, and the Fugitive Slave Law.*[82] This work, dedicated to New York senator William H. Seward, sought to refute the flawed reasoning embraced in the Compromise of 1850.

Seward had scandalized the nation when arguing against any protections for slavery. In a speech on March 11, 1850, the New York senator acknowledged the authority of the United States Constitution. Then he continued: "There is a higher law than the Constitution, which regulates our authority over the domain, and devotes it to the same noble purposes."[83] Apologists for slavery cried foul and attacked Seward in droves. William Hosmer quoted from many philosophers and social theorists to affirm the idea of a higher law, but his book was not a masterpiece of technical argument. Some of the people Hosmer referenced to bolster his view represented rival philosophical traditions. Nevertheless, one more evangelical voice from beyond New England put it all on the line against slavery and for the higher law.

More systematic was the writing and teaching of Joseph Haven (1816–1874). Born in Massachusetts and a graduate of Amherst College and Andover Seminary, Haven would appear to represent the cultured New England clergy more than the self-educated evangelical voices from New

---

82 William Hosmer, *The Higher Law, in its Relations to Civil Government: with Particular Reference to Slavery, and the Fugitive Slave Law* (Auburn, New York: Derby & Miller, 1852).

83 William H. Seward, *Speech of William H. Seward, on the Admission of California. Delivered in the Senate of the United States, March 11, 1850* (Washington, DC: Buell & Blanchard, 1850), 27–28.

York. Yet Joseph Haven remained committed to Congregationalism and is remembered as someone "at once liberal and warmly evangelical."[84] In 1850 he accepted appointment as Professor of Intellectual and Moral Philosophy at Amherst. Gerald F. Vaughn writes: "He essentially exposited the philosophy of Sir William Hamilton, the last of the eminent Scottish common-sense philosophers, and visited Hamilton in Edinburgh in 1854, two years before Hamilton died. Haven took that opportunity in 1854 to also visit Friedrich Wilhelm Joseph Schelling in Berlin, the year Schelling died. Hamilton had helped to bridge the gap between the previously opposing Scottish and German schools of psychological thought."[85] These epistemological sensitivities were given an accessible expression in Haven's 1859 *Moral Philosophy: Including Theoretical and Practical Ethics.*

While Haven's book may appear to be yet one more antebellum text on moral philosophy, the piece demonstrates antislavery ethics come-of-age. Strongly deontological in orientation, Haven gave repetitive attention to defining the "right" and the way this bedrock concept informed moral and even political obligations. Speaking of human legislation, he insisted that, "Law may define and prescribe my rights; it may enforce them, see that they are respected and observed; but it does not, and cannot, create them."[86] He followed by saying, "Both my duties and my rights depend for their existence on *right*; and this again depends, not on society, nor law, but is founded in the eternal and immutable nature of things."[87] It was not always clear what Haven meant by "the eternal and immutable nature of

---

84 Meyer, *The Instructed Conscience*, 151.

85 Gerald F. Vaughn, "Amherst Professor Joseph Haven and His Influence on America's Great Social Critic, Thorstein Veblen," *Historical Journal of Massachusetts* 34, no. 1 (Winter 2006): 44. Elizabeth Flower and Murray G. Murphey remarked that William Hamilton "may be regarded either as the last Scottish realist or as the transitional thinker who begins British Neo-Hegelian Idealism." See Flower and Murphey, *A History of Philosophy in America*, Vol. 1, 245.

86 Joseph Haven, *Moral Philosophy: Including Theoretical and Practical Ethics* (Boston: Gould and Lincoln, 1859), 25.

87 Haven, 26.

things," but it was clear what he did not intend. He would accept no view that reduced the right or rights to some convenient or expedient measure.

The second part of his text addressed practical ethics. Here Haven held forth against slavery in language echoed by others: "It is a wrong, inasmuch as, 1. *It violates the natural rights of man.* It reduces him from a *person to a thing*—than which no greater wrong can be inflicted on humanity. The victim of this injustice is no longer, in the eye of the law, a *man*; he has become a mere thing, has no rights, and, consequently, can suffer no wrong."[88] Such reasoning led to an elaborate analysis of government and a rather startling claim. Since the purpose of the law and government is the public welfare and the protection of rights, when this end is violated, "it may become not only the right, but the duty of the people, to resist the power that proves itself false and recreant to its trust, and to effect a change of government."[89] Joseph Haven did not utter such things lightly, and he qualified his conclusion as the exception, not the rule. Still, his unyielding commitment to human rights—for each and all—echoed throughout the land in the years leading up to Civil War.

Therefore, as many southern intellectuals were developing consequentialist theories of white supremacy by suggesting that rights derive their validity from human legislation, a host of northern deontologists insisted that rights are irreducible and prior to all enactments. The trajectories of these two cultures were not mathematically pure and uncontested, even within the separate regions, but they were identifiable. The irrepressible conflict was as much a philosophical clash as it was anything else.

---

88 Haven, 121.
89 Haven, 277.

Four

NOTHING HALFWAY

A Time to Be Counted

Reverend Asa Mahan was troubled. The pastor of Cincinnati's Sixth Presbyterian Church also served on the board of trustees at Lane Theological Seminary. Lane had been founded in 1829 out among the Walnut Hills area, northeast of Cincinnati. There were very few students—that is until Lyman Beecher, the famous Congregationalist pastor, was named president in 1832. Beecher (1775–1863) had studied at Yale under both Ezra Stiles and Timothy Dwight. He embraced the latter's dynamic leadership but developed a reputation of his own during the early nineteenth century. With Lyman Beecher's appointment as president, students rallied to Cincinnati's Lane Seminary from the East, New York State, the emerging West, and even some parts of the South. Lane was to be an outpost of energetic evangelical ministry down the Ohio River Valley—and beyond.[1]

The location of Lane Theological Seminary near the banks of the Ohio meant it was perched at the great dividing line of North and South, freedom and slavery. Moreover, the Lane students were a unique community. Many were older than most students—some in their middle or late twenties—having been caught up in spiritual revivals from various places and now determined to formalize their theological education. These students

---

1   Edward H. Madden and James E. Hamilton, *Freedom and Grace: The Life of Asa Mahan* (Metuchen, New Jersey: The Scarecrow Press, Inc., 1982), 35–37.

were not naïve, docile teenagers yearning for adulthood. Many already knew themselves well and knew their commitments.

In February 1834, Theodore Weld (1803–1895), perhaps the most experienced and seasoned student of them all, led a discussion regarding the slavery issue. The result was a general consensus (with very few exceptions) among the participants that immediate abolition must be adopted. The students then took to lecturing on the subject, writing for periodicals, and teaching in schools among Cincinnati's African American churches. The trustees of Lane reacted to the student activism with defensive concern. Such forthright abolitionist work could invite retaliation from townspeople and, in their eyes, damage the reputation of the school. After all, they were a mere handful of miles from land where slavery was considered perfectly legal. During the summer of 1834 the trustees appointed a committee to investigate the activities of the students. In August this task force recommended that the student antislavery organization be dissolved, that discussion of the issue be banned, and that the executive board of the trustees should claim the prerogative to dismiss students.[2]

As a member of the Lane Theological Seminary Board of Trustees, Reverend Asa Mahan was more than troubled. He served on the committee that received these authoritarian recommendations, and most of the other trustees were determined to affirm them and crush the student movement. Yet, Asa Mahan and a few others supported the students and dissented from the board. At a meeting held in the Lane Theological Seminary chapel, the student body heard the new restrictions, rose (with the exception of about a dozen), and walked out of Lane Seminary. They were, in effect, homeless, but this would not last long. Soon many of these students entered the Oberlin Collegiate Institute (now Oberlin College), and Asa Mahan took the reins as president at Oberlin.[3]

Asa Mahan was born in 1799 in Vernon, New York. As a child and youth he combined a sensitive personality with a strong determination and

---

2   Madden and Hamilton, *Freedom and Grace: The Life of Asa Mahan*, 37–39.

3   Asa Mahan, *Out of Darkness into Light; or, The Hidden Life Made Manifest* (Boston: Willard Tract Repository, 1876), 114–22.

ambition. He was an intense child. His mother, a rather saintly Presbyterian, once called to her son and said: "The neighbors who visited here yesterday afternoon had a conversation about you. They all agreed that if you should live on to manhood you would become a *very* good or a *very* bad man. There would be nothing half-way about you."[4] When Mahan was seventeen years old, a revival broke out near his home, and he was moved by the preaching. It dawned on the young man that God had always loved him "with a more than parental love."[5] His life changed, and he began a journey from the rigors of Calvinism to an appreciation for the overflowing grace of God and the human ability to respond. He was not some pawn in a world ruled by predestination. He could make a difference.

Asa Mahan dedicated his life to Christ and attended Hamilton College (Clinton, New York). Then he studied at Andover Seminary, graduating in 1827. Mahan married Mary Dix and served various ministries before going to Cincinnati in 1831. Cincinnati's Sixth Presbyterian Church had broken away from its parent body over issues of temperance and abolition, and Asa Mahan's moral views meshed nicely with this reform-minded group. He started to speak out against slavery from the pulpit, which was accepted by his congregation but not the entire community. In 1833 Mahan signed a public call for immediate emancipation of enslaved people, and this was not a popular position at the time.[6] When matters blew apart at Lane Seminary in 1834, Asa Mahan was already established as an advocate for antislavery young people.

The plot to this narrative thickened when famed evangelist Charles G. Finney was enlisted to join Mahan and the "Lane Rebels" (as they were called) in going to Oberlin. Finney (1792–1875) was born in Warren, Connecticut, though his family moved soon thereafter to Oneida County, New York. Later, as young Charles considered a college education he thought seriously about attending Yale but instead chose a course of self-directed

---

4   Asa Mahan, *Fifty Years' Walk with God; or, Reflections on the Completion of My Eighty-Fifth Year* (New York: Willard Tract Repository, 1885), 10–11.

5   Mahan, *Out of Darkness into Light; or, The Hidden Life Made Manifest*, 11.

6   Madden and Hamilton, *Freedom and Grace: The Life of Asa Mahan*, 9–37.

study. In 1818 he joined the law office of Benjamin Wright in Adams, New York. He was an eager student of the law and possessed a strong appetite for learning. He was also a popular and outgoing fellow. Yet something gnawed at Charles Finney's soul. He was no stranger to the church, but he was not an especially committed Christian. By the fall of 1821, he resolved to settle the issue of religious conviction. He spent time alone in prayer and study, hashing things out. After several days of private, often agonizing soul-searching Finney met Christ through an experience that was almost indescribable. He was struck by the truth that God loved him and received him at the deepest level.[7]

Charles Finney's awakening led to some serious decisions regarding the rest of his life. The law interested him greatly, but he felt called to speak and persuade people beyond the courtroom. Later, Finney reminded people of a lawyer making his case. However, the case he argued addressed profound matters of faith. Soon after his conversion, a Deacon Barney dropped by the law office, reminding Finney of a commitment to represent Mr. Barney in court. Finney replied, "Deacon Barney, I have a retainer from the Lord Jesus Christ to plead his cause, and I cannot plead yours."[8] His adventures in preaching began.

Charles Finney engaged in structured theological study under the direction of Rev. George Washington Gale (1789–1861), a Presbyterian pastor. Finney liked Gale but differed with him on many doctrinal issues. Gale was educated at Princeton Seminary and expounded an Old School Calvinism. Somewhat like Asa Mahan, Finney was bothered by the implications of predestination. For one, it seemed to undermine the need for spiritual growth or revival. If our destinies are all pre-established, then why should we seek God? Additionally, how could we live a moral life in response to grace? As Finney viewed things, Gale's theology carried much heavy obligation but made little room for response. He talked with

---

7 Charles G. Finney, *The Memoirs of Charles G. Finney, The Complete Restored Text*, ed. Garth M. Rosell and Richard A. G. Dupuis (Grand Rapids, Michigan: Zondervan Publishing House, 1989), 1–26.

8 Finney, 27.

his tutor about these matters and suggested that Rev. Gale change his perspective. Finney even invoked his legal background. He said that if lawyers employed the logic of Old School pastors (arguing for moral change but denying human ability to respond) they would not win a single case![9] From the standpoint of theological approaches to the will, Asa Mahan and Charles Finney had much in common.

Finney was licensed and ordained by his Presbytery in 1824 and for the next eight years set the frontier on fire with his message of redemption. The Rochester, New York, revival of 1830 was highly publicized and remains a milestone in the history of American evangelicalism. In 1832, Charles Finney, under the sponsorship of New York City's wealthy merchant, Lewis Tappan, began a more settled ministry in Manhattan, but dynamics related to the Lane Seminary controversy soon entered his life.[10]

John J. Shipherd, founder of the Oberlin Collegiate Institute, got wind of the Lane situation and visited the home of Asa Mahan in Cincinnati. A complicated series of negotiations unfolded between the Oberlin authorities and the Lane expatriates. Many of the exiled students would go to Oberlin, but they had conditions. Asa Mahan would have to be appointed president of Oberlin and their own professor, John Morgan, added to the Oberlin faculty. African Americans would have to be admitted, as well, and the Oberlin trustees must promise not to interfere in academic matters. Moreover, the students wanted their leader, Theodore Weld, appointed as Oberlin's professor of theology, but Weld demurred. Instead, he recommended Charles G. Finney. Therefore, in early 1835 many of the Lane Rebels, Asa Mahan, and Charles Finney headed north to begin a storied tenure at the Oberlin Collegiate Institute.[11]

---

9   Finney, 153.
10   Finney, 356–82.
11   Edward H. Madden and James E. Hamilton, *Freedom and Grace: The Life of Asa Mahan*, 44–51.

Reality and Right

The Oberlin team of Charles Finney and Asa Mahan proved to be an immediate success. In Finney the college gained a popular orator and spokesperson for American revivalism. Asa Mahan was a different sort of figure. While certainly a clergyperson with revival experience, Mahan's strongest attributes were exhibited in his teaching of philosophy. He already possessed a reputation for incisive thinking, and as Oberlin's new president, he did not disappoint. With their respective gifts, Finney and Mahan set about instructing students and shaping the ambience of the Oberlin Collegiate Institute. During the last half of the 1830s, they also began translating their theological and philosophical views into published material.

Mahan's first substantial piece was his book, *Scripture Doctrine of Christian Perfection* (1839), but he soon followed with a text on epistemology and ethics. This latter book was really a skeletal collection of lecture material from the previous five years. His *Abstract of a Course of Lectures on Mental & Moral Philosophy* (1840) ran just over three hundred pages. The printing was intended for the exclusive use of students. The first section on "Mental Philosophy" addressed foundational metaphysical and epistemological matters. The second section developed the implications of Mahan's approach for moral philosophy. On the whole, it is a fascinating work, especially so because it reveals influences from other philosophers. Many of these contributing voices were just then becoming known in America.

As an example, one notes the way Samuel Taylor Coleridge informed Mahan's epistemology. The Oberlin president embraced Coleridge's habit of making a distinction between "understanding" and "reason." The first is the faculty of "judging according to sense."[12] The latter is the faculty

---

12 Asa Mahan, *Abstract of a Course of Lectures on Mental & Moral Philosophy* (Oberlin, Ohio: James Steele, 1840), 70. This particular language is taken from S. T. Coleridge, *Aids to Reflection, in the Formation of a Manly Character*, ed. James Marsh (Burlington, Vermont: Chauncey Goodrich, 1829), 137. Coleridge, in turn, attributed this phraseology to Kant.

that apprehends infinite, eternal, and absolute truth. This differentiation was adopted, in various forms, by many Transcendentalists, and in this sense Asa Mahan affirmed the movement.

However, where Transcendentalists tended to consider understanding a second-rate kind of knowledge, Mahan integrated reason and understanding. Moral principles and judgments were approached by him through a coordination of faculties:

> In various processes, however, both faculties are employed, as when we begin with some self-evident principle in morals, for example, and then apply it to facts which lie around us in the world. That theft is wrong, is a first truth of the Reason: but when we apply this principle to a particular act of some individual, and affirm that he has, or has not, in that act, violated this principle, we employ more or less, the Understanding and Judgment, as well as the Reason.[13]

Mahan did sound unmistakably Kantian when applying reason and understanding to human and animal nature. Accordingly, lower beings of creation may exhibit some form of understanding but never pure reason: "Man is an ultimate. The brute is subordinate. In other words, the brute is a means. Man is an end."[14] Once more we hear Asa Mahan echoing the means and ends relationship that played a critical role in Kant's Categorical Imperative.

Mahan's epistemological framework was no accident. Perhaps even more than Coleridge, the Oberlin president relied on the perspective of French philosopher, Victor Cousin. Cousin (1792–1867) was the founder of and advocate for a tradition that became known as "Eclecticism." The name of this school might suggest that Cousin and his colleagues chose various ideas to suit their needs without regard for consistency, but this was not so. Eclecticism was an exceedingly intentional attempt to unite antagonistic philosophies.

---

13 Mahan, 90.
14 Mahan, 94.

The general clash between British and Continental philosophy, especially the divide between experience-based approaches and idealistic approaches, informed Cousin's work. The French thinker wrote a comprehensive commentary on John Locke's *Essay Concerning Human Understanding* that became a landmark text. In America, Caleb Sprague Henry translated Cousin into English and published his critique of Locke under the title, *Elements of Psychology* (1834).[15] By 1836 Henry's translation of Cousin was required reading among the Oberlin curriculum.

Mahan endorsed Cousin's approach to what was typically called "the origin of ideas." In a manner similar to American Transcendentalists, Cousin recognized the division between the empirical or sensual school and the ideal school, but Cousin thought these two were, in effect, opposite sides of one coin. The second chapter of Cousin's commentary reveals the details of this thinking, and Asa Mahan stood on the same ground when discussing the way humans develop particular ideas.

Mahan's *Abstract* invoked Cousin without much qualification. The Oberlin president claimed that necessary and universal truths cannot be the objects of experience, but they can be known through experience. This fine sifting of distinctions called for an extended and accessible explanation, and Mahan was happy to offer one. At bottom was Cousin's typology of describing ideas in either "logical" or "chronological" terms.

Asa Mahan explained that when an idea logically supposes another, the latter is called the antecedent of the first. He illustrated this by saying that the idea of "body" can only be conceived on the condition of admitting "space." Therefore, space is the logical antecedent of body, and this illustrates the strength of Kant's transcendental school. Yet an idea is seen to be chronologically antecedent of another when, in the actual experience of the human mind, the former precedes the latter. Mahan claimed that

---

15 Victor Cousin, *Elements of Psychology: Included in a Critical Examination of Locke's Essay on the Human Understanding*, trans. C. S. Henry (Hartford: Cooke and Company, 1834).

experiential thoughts are the chronological antecedents of necessary, universal ideas, and this illustrates the strength of Locke's sensual school.[16]

The insistence that universal ideas are apprehended *from* experience but not dependent *on* experience was crucial. It drove Asa Mahan's articulation of moral philosophy. He adopted an uncompromisingly deontological theory that, like the ethic of Immanuel Kant, defended transcendental, universal law. Yet unlike the ethic of Kant, the moral philosophy of Mahan asserted that universal law could be known through intuitive experience, not solely by abstract processes. In short, Asa Mahan blended Kantian idealism and Scottish intuitionism.

Mahan's form of "eclecticism" required close reading. When discussing the conceptions of right and wrong he was unequivocal. The ideas of right and wrong are "universal. Moral law knows of no exception."[17] However, while Mahan had deep appreciation for Kant's application of "universalizability," he tended to sound more like Thomas Reid when it came to receiving the moral law. Later in his *Abstract*, he wrote:

> The moral philosopher assumes the validity of the moral faculty in two respects;
>
> (1.) The capability of the intellectual faculties to determine the relations actually existing among creatures and that of the conscience to affirm the duties arising out of these relations when determined, and,
>
> (2.) That what the moral faculty necessarily affirms to be right or wrong, is so in fact.[18]

The Oberlin president asserted the moral law's authority beyond experience while describing its reception through experience.

In the end, Asa Mahan rested his ethic on an oft-repeated statement: "The fundamental requirement of the moral law, as we have seen in preceding lectures, is this: Every object presented to our contemplation, is

---

16 Mahan, *Abstract of a Course of Lectures on Mental & Moral Philosophy*, 97–100.
17 Mahan, 193.
18 Mahan, 239.

to be esteemed by us according to its intrinsic worth."[19] Such language amounted to a declaration that the world around us has objective value, and people, in particular, possess an inherent worth. Mahan linked this conviction to the Scriptural law of love for God and neighbor.[20]

There were very real political implications to this thinking. Ideas of right and wrong that are eternal and absolute, even if gleaned from experience, demonstrate that human rights are logically prior to human law. Near the end of his lectures, Mahan wrote that, "Government does not, in the discharge of its proper functions, create rights, but protects them."[21] Therefore, Asa Mahan stood in a long line of those deontologists who understood rights to have their own status. They were not dependent upon the approval of legislative bodies or political leaders for their validity. They were a part of being human.

It would not be quite accurate to say that Mahan's *Abstract of a Course of Lectures on Mental & Moral Philosophy* telegraphed everything about his thought for the next fifty years, but it came close to doing so. Additionally, this outline of both metaphysics/epistemology and ethics demonstrated an early appreciation for German and French philosophy. There was much of Scottish Realism that remained in the soul of Asa Mahan. Yet, his residual respect for experience always pointed to the necessary and unchanging.

The Case for Benevolence at Oberlin

Because Asa Mahan's *Abstract* was never circulated widely, Charles Finney became the first to release a recognized and codified Christian theology from Oberlin. While not a specific text on moral philosophy, Finney's *Lectures on Systematic Theology* (two volumes, 1846 and 1847) addressed the subject of ethics at various intervals, and it was evident that he embraced a modified teleological or consequentialist system.

---

19 Mahan, 257.
20 Mahan, 257.
21 Mahan, 276.

Charles Finney's ethic stood within the New England tradition of Edwards, Hopkins, and others who emphasized "benevolence." Very early in his text, the Oberlin professor wrote that, "Wisdom consists in the choice of the best ends, and in the use of the most appropriate means to accomplish those ends."[22] He understood the controlling goal of humanity to be the highest well-being of God and creation: "This is the *Ultimate End*—the good of *God* and our *neighbor*."[23] When analyzing "the foundation of obligation" (a phrase employed by many philosophers) Finney insisted that moral duty be derived from this one ultimate goal: "*Lastly, I come to the consideration of the practical bearings of what I regard as the true theory of the foundation of moral obligation, namely that the highest well-being of God and of the Universe is the sole foundation of moral obligation.*"[24] Overall, it is not hard to read Charles Finney as a descendant of New England theology, but this view demands some qualification.

Finney did work to distance himself from the callous calculations of many consequentialists by stressing the will (as opposed to exclusive focus on results). He went to great lengths in drawing this distinction between intention and subsequent acts. Fundamentally, the concepts of right and wrong referred to intention throughout Finney's ethic:

> It is a saying as common as men are, and as true as common, that men are to be judged by their motives, that is, by their designs, intentions. It is impossible for us not to assent to this truth. If a man intend evil, though perchance he may do us good, we do not excuse him, but hold him guilty of the crime which he intended.

---

22 Charles G. Finney, *Lectures on Systematic Theology, Embracing Lectures on Moral Government* (Oberlin, Ohio: James M. Fitch, 1846), 20. The best purely philosophical comparison of Asa Mahan and Charles Finney is James E. Hamilton, "A Comparison of the Moral Theories of Charles Finney and Asa Mahan" (PhD diss., State University of New York, 1972).

23 Finney, 57.

24 Finney, 148.

So if he intended to do us good, and perchance do us evil, we do not, and cannot condemn him.[25]

This conviction concealed one catch. The intention's moral value was still identified with its relation to an end, which reigned supreme.

Finney used this distinction between intention and result in an attempt to distance himself from the utilitarianism of William Paley. The Oberlin professor described both intention and performance of moral acts this way. The former was a determination of choice, the latter execution of the behavior chosen. Finney asserted that the inward act of intention could not be justified in reference to any utility. Such a justification would, indeed, spell some type of utilitarianism. In contrast, he maintained that an intention was good or bad in relation to the intrinsic value of the end chosen. It was not good or bad because the act of choosing produced desired consequences.

If today's reader has some difficulty following Charles Finney here, she or he is not alone. Many in his day struggled to grasp the meaning of these distinctions. There is a fine line between making insightful differentiations and simply splitting hairs. It remains unclear how Finney should be judged regarding this question.

We cannot fault Finney for trying, even if his argument seemed strained, and sometimes it was exceedingly strained. He was not afraid to make his point in great detail:

> The inquiry then, is it expedient? in respect to outward action, is always proper; for upon this condition does obligation to outward action turn. But in respect to ultimate intention or the choice of an ultimate end, an inquiry into the expediency of this choice or intention is never proper, the obligation being founded alone upon the perceived and intrinsic value of the end, and the obligation being without any condition whatever, except the possession of the powers of moral agency, with the perception of the end upon

25 Finney, 36–37.

which intention ought to terminate, namely, the good of universal being.[26]

Finney's tortured prose did not help his cause, and the style was less than direct, at least in part, because he seemed to want things both ways. Still, he claimed that his distinctions properly set him apart from Paley's utilitarianism.

Even if we accept that Charles Finney was not a utilitarian in the formal sense, his ethic did remain in consequentialist territory. Additionally, Finney made an explicit argument against deontological approaches. The latter were lumped together under a criticism of "rightarianism."[27] As we have seen, teleological or consequentialist systems were identified with a search for "the good," and deontological systems were identified with an emphasis on "the right." It was partly a matter of honest definition and partly a use of derisive language to call deontological thinking "rightarianism." Consequentialists (such as Finney) characterized these theories as unreasonable, even arbitrary and unyielding.

Finney understood deontologists to claim that in choosing an ultimate end, they were choosing something "for its own intrinsic value . . . and not as a means or condition of any other end."[28] This was not inaccurate, but it was a conviction that received his criticism. The Oberlin professor insisted that any proper ethic must choose some supremely valuable end, and that this end must be the highest good or well-being of God and of the universe. For Charles Finney, the moral law served a teleological or consequentialist purpose.[29]

There was even some suggestion that deontological thinking might be dangerous. Charles Finney saw it as extreme and inflexible, and such views could lead to conflict when larger, social issues were considered. He wrote that, "This philosophy tends naturally to fanaticism. Conceiving

---

26 Finney, 137.
27 Finney, 76–89.
28 Finney, 77.
29 Finney, 78.

as it does of right as distinct from and often opposed to benevolence, it scoffs or rails at the idea of inquiring what the highest good evidently demands."[30] Of course, Finney stepped into the inevitable quandary that those with privilege inherit. Who exactly should decide what the highest good demands? Those with power? Those who dominate established institutions? Many abusive systems have been protected by those claiming to be reasonable.

Charles Finney identified the modern origins of rightarianism with the thought of Kant, Cousin, and Coleridge. He even quoted from Cousin's *Elements of Psychology*: "Do right for the sake of the right, or rather, will the right for the sake of the right. Morality has to do with the intentions."[31] Given that Asa Mahan named Kant, Cousin, and Coleridge as inspiration for his moral philosophy, it is easy to anticipate a clash between the Oberlin president and the Oberlin professor of theology.

Finney hinted at this developing conflict when he admitted that some rightarians were very close to home. He was blunt in his opposition, but he seemed to honor a proper separation of ideas from persons. When speaking of rightarians, he added that, "Many of them I regard as among the excellent of the earth, and I am happy to count them among my dearest and most valued friends."[32] Yet it is difficult to assess this statement, and it leaves some lingering questions. For one, it follows a claim that most deontologists (or rightarians) did not practice their odious theories. Were deontologists well-meaning fools who left their stated principles behind when acting? Did this make them eligible for Charles Finney's friendship? Or did he genuinely respect those who disagreed with him? It is hard to say.

Because Asa Mahan endorsed a deontological ethic, it is easy to typecast him as one who could accept no compromise, and there is much truth in this description of both his ethic and his personality. However, Charles

---

30 Finney, 140.

31 Finney, 77. See also Victor Cousin, *Elements of Psychology*, 2nd ed. (New York: Gould & Newman, 1838), 162.

32 Finney, 143.

Finney's argument for a moral philosophy that claimed to be interested in the overall good did not make him a flawless person. Finney had his likes and dislikes, his strong opinions (even if they sought cover in "benevolence"). The Oberlin Collegiate Institute was known for espousing settled convictions on a variety of matters. Some of these convictions were drawn from the thinking and teaching of Asa Mahan, but some of them were drawn from that of Charles G. Finney. One can see the self as a protector of the good and presume to know that good in less than enlightened ways. One can see the self as a protector of the right and overlook the ideas of others. Moral philosophy and social action in the middle nineteenth century were tricky business. This was so for many reasons, not the least being the way these issues attached themselves to specific personalities.

Those who hold ethical theory in disdain, because it is too ethereal, demonstrate a serious lack of self-understanding, at best—and perhaps even disingenuousness. More often than not, impatience with moral theory indicates that someone is not getting his or her way. Even those who attempt to evaluate theory from some ostensibly pure position cannot help but step into a larger narrative. Theoretical constructs matter, but context and imprecision will force themselves among the conversation. We might as well be honest about things and get on with exploring the complicated and compelling story of ethics in antebellum America. Few versions of this story are more technical than the conflict between Asa Mahan and Charles Finney, and few reflect the intrigue of personality more than this same disagreement.

Into the Open

Charles Finney's two-volume *Systematic Theology* was rolled out over 1846 and 1847. Asa Mahan's formal text on ethics appeared in 1848. His *Science of Moral Philosophy* dropped the format of the *Abstract* and did not include much on epistemology. It did, however, flesh out the theoretical dynamics of his deontological view and apply these principles to practical ethics. The 1848 book was also more explicit in criticizing Finney's approach than Finney had been when dismissing Mahan's type of theory.

Yet it is not quite fair to say that Asa Mahan initiated the debate. Charles Finney was more passive-aggressive in his argument, but he should not be let off the hook entirely. He knew what he was implying when he attacked rightarianism.

Subsequent assessments have typically characterized Asa Mahan as the more direct and assertive participant in this disagreement, but Charles Finney seemed to bait his colleague and then deny culpability. In any case, Mahan's *Science of Moral Philosophy* devoted thirty pages to an open commentary on Finney's ethic.[33] The Oberlin president was unmistakably clear in his argument "against the theory of Professor Finney, and in favor of the opposite theory, the direct and positive testimony of universal consciousness."[34] The terminology of "universal consciousness" may seem vague. In one manner, it might reference the moral sense and how we have immediate insight regarding right and wrong. In another manner, it probably suggests something more Kantian, truths that are beyond sense and human calculation. Overall, though, these nuances were consistent with Mahan's earlier blending of Scottish and German thought.

Especially grating to Asa Mahan was Charles Finney's assertion that morality could be reduced to a unified measurement of means and ends. He conceded that the good of being may be a reason for intentions of a certain kind, but he also stated that there are other objects (for example, virtue and sin, character and desert) which provide ultimate reasons for specific acts of the will or intentions. To put it more plainly, happiness or the good of being cannot subordinate all other reasons for acting. Mahan summed up his overall criticism this way: "According to Professor Finney, there is but one object in existence the apprehension of which intrinsically necessitates acts of will, to wit, the good of being."[35] According to the Oberlin president, there are many objects that, when apprehended, require acts of will.

---

33 Mahan, *Science of Moral Philosophy,* 94–123.
34 Mahan, 106.
35 Mahan, 98.

By this point in Mahan's analysis, there was very little to set the conversation apart from a general critique of consequentialism. Yet he pushed forward with more detailed and particular dissection of Charles Finney's theory. The most emphatic and perhaps significant argument of Mahan denied that Finney had affected any real separation from utilitarianism. The Oberlin president could not buy Professor Finney's insistence that a focus on ultimate intentions prevented his ethic from being utilitarian. Mahan countered that when happiness or well-being become the controlling end, even subordinate intentions function according to utilitarian values: "If the intelligence does require or prohibit intentions for no other reasons than as a condition or a means of happiness, this is the doctrine of Utility, as maintained by all its advocates."[36] We may question whether Mahan collapsed Finney's theory into some manageable category so that he might dismiss his colleague's position. Then again, Finney did struggle with consistency.

Asa Mahan probably stepped over the line in one of his concluding criticisms. He suggested that Finney's theory might give one a poorly developed moral character. He did not say that his Oberlin colleague was deficient in character. He even claimed that many who affirmed Finney's theory were, personally, of sterling constitution. However, the Oberlin president understood this virtue to be present "in spite of their theory, not in consequence of it."[37] Such philosophical sass may have been unbecoming, but it closely resembled Charles Finney's attack on those who held deontological views. After all, Finney stated that the admirable qualities of rightarians demonstrated the way they seldom employed their fanatical principles.[38]

The conflict was now out in the open, and there was no way that Asa Mahan's critique would go unnoticed by Charles Finney. We cannot determine for sure the detail of conversation between them regarding this intramural squabble, but eventually Finney revealed his feelings. Mahan was

---

36 Mahan, 99.
37 Mahan, 112.
38 Finney, *Lectures on Systematic Theology*, 143.

president of Oberlin between 1835 and 1850, so the *Moral Philosophy* is remembered as one of his last contributions from the College. To make matters worse, the president did not leave Oberlin on good terms with the faculty. Finney was definitely irritated, and in 1851 he shared his displeasure with a friend:

> Have you read my Dear Br. Mahan's Moral Philosophy? If so you have noted the sad confusion of his mind on the question of the *foundation of Obligation. . . .* I was obliged to write a review of it *for the use of the students,* which I have in manuscript, but dislike to publish because I so much love Br. M. and because of my relations to him. . . . I feared that Dear Br. M. would fall into confusion just as he did because in his former treatise he had done so. But I am sorry to say that on this question his confusion rather increases than otherwise.[39]

Subsequent observers have differed as to whether Finney or Mahan presented the clearest system of moral philosophy. Mahan's ability to synthesize Kant, Coleridge, and Cousin (not to mention, Thomas Reid) made him a formidable thinker. Yet this did not persuade every reader. Finney spoke from an established New England school, but he managed to make that tradition rather confusing when addressing the finer points. Perhaps most dubious was Finney's denial that his theory had anything to do with utilitarianism.

By 1870 Asa Mahan had moved on to creative ventures in theology. His controversial text, *The Baptism of the Holy Ghost,* included a passage that sought to smooth troubled waters. Mahan (by then at Adrian College in Michigan) suggested that the Holy Spirit does not make one infallible. Honest disciples can disagree and still learn from one another: "On a very few questions in Moral Philosophy and Theology, Brother Finney and myself have arrived at opposite conclusions. Yet each has the same

---

39 Quoted in Madden and Hamilton, *Freedom and Grace: The Life of Asa Mahan,*
    82. The original is found in Charles G. Finney to James Morison, January 5, 1851,
    the Moir Collection, Mitchell Library, Glasgow.

assurance as before, that the other is 'full of faith, and of the Holy Ghost,' and never were our mutual love and esteem stronger than now. We differ just where minds under the influence of the purest integrity, and the highest form of divine illumination, are liable to differ."[40] Perhaps, but when it came to admitting a rift, we might not help concluding that both Finney and Mahan protested too much. This was no minor disagreement.

Later Benjamin Breckinridge Warfield of Princeton named the obvious. Writing as the twentieth century opened, the old Calvinist (no fan of either Mahan or Finney) poked fun at the way the Oberlin duo tried to cover their dispute in platitudes: "It would almost seem as if it were a virtue to differ on these things."[41] Warfield was a quotable curmudgeon, and even though his lineage was anything but progressive regarding human rights, he sided with Mahan when it came to moral theory. He labeled Finney's consequentialism "no morality at all."[42] This judgment reflected Princeton's ancestral conflict with Yale around matters of theology and moral philosophy, and it was no unqualified endorsement of Asa Mahan's work.

Over the years, interpretive layers of scholarship have tended to categorize the difference between Asa Mahan and Charles Finney in less technical terms. Mahan, the more precise of the two, was the nearest thing to a professional philosopher among the Old Northwest. Finney, the evangelist turned professor, remained committed to saving souls. All else was of secondary importance. Mahan could afford to state moral matters unequivocally, and he could insist on universal application of principles in varied cases. Finney had to consider consequences, the way his theory would help or hinder a preaching ministry. Even Edward H. Madden concluded that: "Asa Mahan was Oberlin's strongest advocate of organized

---

40 Asa Mahan, *The Baptism of the Holy Ghost* (New York: Palmer & Hughes, 1870), 125.
41 Benjamin Breckinridge Warfield, *Studies in Perfectionism*, ed. Samuel G. Craig (Phillipsburg, New Jersey: Presbyterian and Reformed Publishing Company, 1958), 125.
42 Warfield, 125.

reform. Finney, as an evangelist and revivalist, felt that there is only one basic reform from which all others naturally flow."[43] According to this analysis, Charles Finney's concern for human rights was no less authentic, simply less direct. Convert society, and justice would follow.

As with many interpretive approaches, there is much to commend this view of Mahan and Finney. Yet, Charles Finney was not shy about entering the world of complex reasoning, even if he mishandled aspects of his argument, and Asa Mahan was not indifferent about religious revivals. In fact, Mahan held his own when it came to proclaiming the gospel. The two may have repaired their friendship as the years went by, but their disagreement was not a mirage. It was real, and it was *philosophical*.

Such a difference regarding first principles was bound to reveal itself in the social witness expressed by these two. Their contrasting ethical constructs shaped, at least partially, their contrasting approaches to societal issues. Again, theory matters, and it matters because it is inextricably linked to people and practice.

The Consequences of Consequentialism

Charles G. Finney made his mark on more than one social reform movement. Several decades ago, evangelical scholars argued that the egalitarian nature of Finney's revivals, along with his involvement in coeducation at Oberlin, made him a prime force in the early and mid-nineteenth-century struggle for women's rights.[44] In contrast to some of Oberlin's professors, Finney encouraged women students to join in classroom dialogue and recitation.[45] Even so, the issue of abolition absorbed more of his attention.

Later in life, while writing his memoirs, Finney recollected the year 1835. He explained the conditions under which he agreed to leave his full-time responsibilities in New York and become a professor at Oberlin. As

---

43 Madden, *Civil Disobedience and Moral Law in Nineteenth-Century American Philosophy*, 70.

44 See especially the treatment by Nancy A. Hardesty, *Women Called to Witness: Evangelical Feminism in the 19th Century* (Nashville: Abingdon Press, 1984).

45 Hardesty, 92–93.

told by the great evangelist, he had insisted that the faculty retain primary authority over governance of the college and that African Americans be admitted on terms equal to anyone else.[46] The first point gave the faculty tremendous powers and would become an item of contention with the Mahan presidency. Yet the second point deserves particular attention. Finney had an ongoing concern for the plight of people of color, and this interest was often expressed in both speaking and writing. However, a closer examination of his views and his actions regarding race reveals a more complicated story.

The year that Charles Finney began teaching in Oberlin also marked the release of his *Lectures on Revivals of Religion* (1835). This book served as a kind of field manual regarding best methods for leading revivals, and Finney presented in systematic fashion the principles for promoting renewal. While focusing on such spiritual practices as prayer, preaching, and organizing the converted, he also recognized that any awakening was only as good as its ethical foundation. He joined others in a great evangelical movement for social improvement and claimed that sin could suffocate revivals. Finney insisted that, "Revivals are hindered when ministers and *churches take wrong ground in regard to any question involving human rights.*"[47] Here he had slavery especially in mind.

Finney pointed out that the well-known figure, John Newton, continued his occupation as a trader of enslaved persons following conversion. However, as Finney told the tale, Newton subsequently experienced such a searing of conscience that he could no longer go on as both a Christian and a trafficker in people. To remain in that diabolical occupation would have ruined his faith. Likewise, Finney argued, American Christians would have to renounce slavery once and for all: "Their silence can no longer be accounted for upon the principle of ignorance, and that they have never had their attention turned to the subject. Consequently, the silence of Christians upon the subject is virtually saying *that they do not*

---

46 Finney, *The Memoirs of Charles G. Finney, The Complete Restored Text*, 380.

47 Charles G. Finney, *Lectures on Revivals of Religion*, 2nd ed. (New York: Leavitt, Lord & Co., 1835), 265.

consider slavery as a sin. The truth is, it is a subject upon which they cannot be silent without guilt."[48] As Charles Finney entered his labors among the Oberlin community, he made it plain that Christians must support the abolitionist movement. The authenticity of religious revival depended on such candor and commitment.

Historians have taken note of these statements by Finney and have acknowledged that his form of evangelicalism was rather prophetic, for its day. This was generally so, but when the abolitionist movement began to polarize the nation, he experienced doubts. As early as 1836 Finney expressed concern that an overly confrontational stand would only serve to push the nation into civil war. Lane Seminary "rebel" Theodore Weld was a close associate of Finney and had been led to Christ by the evangelist in the 1820s. Yet Finney shared his reservations with Weld regarding the direction of the antislavery cause: "Br. Weld, is it not true, at least do you not fear it is, that we are in our present course going fast into a civil war? Will not our present movements in abolition result in that? Shall we not ere long be obliged to take refuge in a military despotism?"[49] The cause was certainly noble, but the price appeared remarkably high. A theologian and revivalist who made the general well-being of God and neighbor primary would have a difficult time justifying civil conflict. Finney seemed to lack the temperament and the theoretical justification for a strident campaign against slavery.

Many of Charles Finney's contemporaries embraced him as a genuine supporter of the antislavery message, but the residual unwillingness to push matters toward a perceived extreme damaged his reputation among some abolitionists. Finney's relationship with New York City business leader and Oberlin benefactor, Lewis Tappan, was particularly marred by disagreement over abolitionist principles. Tappan threatened to withdraw financial support from the Ohio school if Finney did not take a more

---

48 Finney, 266.

49 Gilbert H. Barnes and Dwight L. Dumond, eds., *Letters of Theodore Dwight Weld, Angelina Grimke Weld, and Sarah Grimke, 1822–1844*, 2 vols. (New York and London: D. Appleton-Century Company, Inc., 1934), 1:318.

aggressive stand against slavery and for racial equality.[50] The former demand of Tappan left some room for inquiry. How was Finney to be more assertive regarding the sin of slavery? The second demand, however, reflected troubling practices in Finney's ministry.

Charles Finney somehow managed to convince himself that condemning slavery did not necessarily require full integration. He denied communion to those who held others in slavery, but seating in his church segregated people by race.[51] Lewis Tappan and his brother Arthur did not understand how the evangelist could appear to support abolition and simultaneously prohibit integration. When they confronted Finney with this inconsistency, his only defense was a wordy rationalization. In a letter to Arthur Tappan, the evangelist argued:

> You err in supposing that the principle of abolition and amalgamation are identical. . . . Abolition is a question of flagrant and unblushing wrong. A direct and outrageous violation of fundamental right. The other is a question of prejudice that does not necessarily deprive any man of any positive right. . . . Now it appears to me that to make these two questions identical is to give the opposers of abolition a great advantage over us in point of argument and that to bring forward and insist upon amalgamation just now would do infinite mischief to our cause.[52]

Finney's way of speaking about rights here should give us pause. Evidently, the good of humanity demanded an end to slavery but not equal opportunity for participation and leadership. Negatively speaking, he did not want integration to raise the kind of controversy that would threaten

---

50 Lewis A. Drummond, *Charles Grandison Finney and the Birth of Modern Evangelism* (London: Hodder and Stoughton, 1983), 203.

51 Michael O. Emerson and Christian Smith, *Divided by Faith: Evangelical Religion and the Problem of Race in America* (Oxford: Oxford University Press, 2000), 33. See also Lewis A. Drummond, *Charles Grandison Finney and the Birth of Modern Evangelism*, 204.

52 Charles G. Finney to Arthur Tappan, April 30, 1836, reel 3, *Papers*, Recordak Corportation, Cleveland, Ohio.

some purportedly higher cause (a typically consequentialist form of logic). Yet this also opened the door to understanding the general welfare as something that must be controlled by privileged people. Those with power reserved the right to determine how abolition would be implemented.

Charles Finney's attitudes and limitations can be viewed from many angles, but we ought to note that a very real philosophical question was at stake. The evangelist shared his core conviction in the following terms: "As a matter of philosophy, it is certainly unwise and unphilosophical to distract the publick attention with two questions at the same time instead of one."[53] From his perspective, Finney not only feared the general ill that might attend a forcing of integration. He believed that to present abolition and integration as twin aims would confuse social sentiment regarding right and wrong. How he managed to convince himself of this claim is not exactly clear.

Writing at the beginning of the present century, Michael O. Emerson and Christian Smith raised serious objections to any who would see in Charles Finney an admirable witness for justice. They acknowledged the evangelist's forthright stand against slavery but maintained that his failure to defend equal participation left a racist legacy. It is hard to disagree with this criticism. Charles Finney was not necessarily the mid-nineteenth-century hero desired by some contemporary evangelicals. However, Emerson and Smith fall into the predictable pattern of contrasting Finney and other evangelicals with less religiously orthodox abolitionists, such as Boston's William Lloyd Garrison. Garrison is called the leader of "more radical and largely non-evangelical abolitionists."[54] Finney is considered the archetype of evangelicals, who were "more moderate."[55] It is a familiar typology, but it has serious limitations.

One need not defend Charles Finney to argue against this interpretation. There were evangelicals who could be described as "radical"

---

53 Finney.

54 Michael O. Emerson and Christian Smith, *Divided by Faith: Evangelical Religion and the Problem of Race in America*, 32.

55 Emerson and Smith, 32.

regarding both slavery and equality (full integration and participation). Garrison has become the default darling when defining radicalism, and we should begin asking ourselves what this means. Does a penchant for unorthodox religious beliefs make an abolitionist more "radical"? Garrison was notorious for refraining from political involvement due to his sweeping condemnation of the system. Does opting out make one more "radical"? Perhaps today's labels—"radical" and "moderate"—reflect something of our current assumptions about the secular left and religious traditions. Asa Mahan maintained both an evangelical faith and a radical commitment to equality—beyond the abolition of slavery. Maybe it is time to consider new paradigms of interpretation.

For "Afflicted Humanity"

Asa Mahan, while sharing an overall reform perspective with Charles Finney, differed substantially in the way he related to particular issues. Finney's disposition and moral theory led to compromising behavior. This was not the case with Mahan. The Oberlin president acted as the most assertive advocate for women's rights on campus and participated in the Underground Railroad.[56] He embraced the role of moral leadership and seemed to be one half step ahead of others around him. Mahan's prophetic persona cast a large shadow, and he was thought to be self-righteous by some. There is no denying that the president possessed ample confidence when it came to issues of right and wrong. He seldom equivocated, and the comprehensive sweep of his convictions could be interpreted as excessive by less demanding souls. Still, some of this judgment is probably a caricature, handed down by admirers of Charles Finney.[57]

---

56 Madden and Hamilton, *Freedom and Grace: The Life of Asa Mahan*, 85, 89–94.

57 Charles Finney succeeded Mahan as president at Oberlin in 1850. The comment of Charles E. Hambrick-Stowe is typical: "When President Finney chaired faculty and trustees meetings, his leadership contrasted markedly with that of Asa Mahan. Instead of directing decisions and events with an autocratic hand, he moderated meetings in a consensus-building style." See Charles E. Hambrick-Stowe,

Later in life Mahan acknowledged the way his beliefs put him at risk with others. He recalled an intentional decision to handle controversial matters with clarity and firmness: "The principle settled upon was this: Every such question should be determined, not at all with reference to what is popular, or to what is approved within the circle of my sect or party in Church or State, but with a simple reference to what is true, right, and just in itself, and to what the permanent interests of the Church and the public demand."[58] This approach had costs. Mahan admitted so. Looking back he mused: "By a steady and inflexible adherence to such a principle, I should not, in all probability, as I clearly saw, be well adjusted to popular favour."[59] Some of Asa Mahan's conflict with others was certainly self-inflicted, but a great deal of it came with his unwillingness to go along to get along.

During his presidency Mahan debated many well-known figures who visited campus for an exchange of ideas.[60] Most recalled his deportment as respectful and his rhetoric as directed at the arguments he opposed, not the people presenting them. Still, he was remembered for standing his ground. One cause close to his heart was that of coeducation. Charles Finney expressed support for women students, but Mahan gave the issue consistent attention. He kept up the pressure for offering equal opportunity to both women and men. During the middle 1840s, two especially gifted students made their mark at Oberlin, and Mahan demonstrated determined advocacy for their work. Lucy Stone and Antoinette Brown were both strong people with intellectual skills that demanded respect. In 1847 the president proposed that Stone read her own essay at that year's commencement exercises, but he was overruled by the faculty. The next

---

Charles G. Finney and the Spirit of American Evangelicalism (Grand Rapids, Michigan: William B. Eerdmans Publishing Company, 1996), 268.

58 Asa Mahan, *Autobiography: Intellectual, Moral, and Spiritual* (London: T. Woolmer, 1882), 161.

59 Mahan, 161.

60 Madden and Hamilton, *Freedom and Grace: The Life of Asa Mahan*, 86–87.

year he attempted to have his daughter, Anna, read her essay. This too was voted down.[61]

Antoinette Brown took up the cause of equality through meticulous biblical scholarship. She presented an argument in favor of women's speech, which caused much debate among the campus community. Asa Mahan backed her position with supportive enthusiasm. Brown's "Reminiscences of Early Oberlin" recalled those days: "Pres. Mahan was in office for two years after I entered college. He was liberal and criticized on that account. I used to air my pet opinions in my compositions and one of them was an exegesis on St. Paul's teaching—suffer not women to speak in the church. Pres. Mahan heard of it and sent for it and had it printed in the next edition of the Oberlin Review. The first article I ever had printed."[62] The complete argument appeared as "Exegesis of 1 Corinthians, XIV., 34, 35; and 1 Timothy, II., 11, 12" in volume 4, number 3 of *The Oberlin Quarterly Review* (January 1849).

However, Mahan's lasting legacy regarding abolition and race made an impression all its own. The president's commencement address of August 1841 articulated a platform for consistent social justice advocacy. He underscored the urgency of the antislavery fight and warned his audience of the temptation to compromise. He even presented an extended summation of the tactics used to oppose the right: "We may also understand the reason of the manner in which these reforms are opposed, when opposition is made to them. As a matter of fact, they are never opposed as being in principle wrong. The apologist for the evils which these movements are designed to correct, always begins his apology by assuring the public, that he is as much opposed to these evils as any man living."[63] Why then such resistance? According to Mahan, the cause was undermined by those who cried: "O the movement is untimely! Its discussion now will

---

61 Madden and Hamilton, 91.

62 Antoinette Brown Blackwell, "Reminiscences of Early Oberlin," February 1918, The Schlesinger Library, Radcliffe College, A-77, Folder 1.

63 Asa Mahan, "President Mahan's Address," *The Oberlin Evangelist* 3, no. 24 (November 24, 1841): 187.

produce great and endless agitation of the public mind!"[64] Asa Mahan was many things, but he was not timid. He called out those who avoided issues simply because powerful people would rather ignore them. We should also note that this same address linked the words of the Declaration of Independence and the "eternal and immutable difference" between people and things. The Kantian distinction was never far from his mind.[65]

Mahan extended the discussion on social reform through an eight-part series, published in *The Oberlin Evangelist* between February and August of 1844. At one point, he made a claim that can only be described as "categorical." According to President Mahan, "No man is a reformer from principle, in any one branch of reform, who is not, in spirit, and from principle, a *universal* reformer. In other words, no man ever, from principle, aims at the correction of any one evil, who will suffer any other acknowledged evil to pass uncorrected."[66] Additionally, a few paragraphs above this statement, Mahan reiterated yet again: "We have, for example, the anti-slavery reform resting upon the principle that there is an immutable difference between a person and a thing, that the conversion of moral agents into 'chattels personal' is eternally wrong, and destructive to the dearest rights and interests of humanity."[67] In a later installment of the series he called the church a universal reform society.[68] While Charles Finney worried about the church's reputation and standing in polite "society," Asa Mahan saw the church as a society intended for love and justice.

The president's unqualified statements may seem removed from specific action, but for Mahan, ideas and action were of one whole. He often spoke of very particular situations and examples in the quest for right. Near the end of his life, he replied to racist arguments by invoking his

---

64 Mahan, 187.

65 Mahan, 187.

66 Asa Mahan, "Reform," *The Oberlin Evangelist* 6, no. 10 (May 8, 1844): 76.

67 Mahan. This very same distinction was emphasized in his essay for *The Oberlin Evangelist* 6, no. 6 (March 13, 1844): 45.

68 Mahan, *The Oberlin Evangelist* (July 17, 1844): 117.

experience as an educator. He recalled a young survivor of the notorious *Amistad* brutality who studied at the Oberlin Collegiate Institute: "As a general scholar, few exceeded her, and none in mathematics."[69] This kind of particularity was not a tokenism, unaware of systemic forces. In Asa Mahan's universe, each and every person mattered. Near the end of his 1846 *Oberlin Quarterly Review* essay regarding fundamental principles, Mahan shifted his prose from explication of theory to story.

He told of a large conference among social reformers, where representatives from various societies met to coordinate strategy. The gathering was held in Cincinnati, and when it was over, participants boarded stagecoaches for several destinations. Some going to Lexington, Kentucky, met the stage and found that it already had one passenger, an African American woman. Instead of entering the vehicle with courtesy and kindness, the boarding travelers made a spectacle of themselves in order to avoid sitting near her. One prominent member of the clergy announced, "If there is an abolitionist here, *there* is a seat for him."[70] The group of white travelers joined in cruel laughter, and the woman endured outrageous indignity. Infuriated, Mahan remarked that such racist behavior demonstrated how those supposed reformers were entirely devoid of credibility.

He also employed rather curious language to describe the rudely treated passenger: "In her, afflicted humanity was represented in one of its most unprotected forms."[71] Asa Mahan always revered the uniqueness of each person. At the same time, he saw in people the representative value of humanity. We get a hint of this dynamic when he talked about Oberlin's mission. Many derided the school simply because it stood before the world "as the equal and impartial friend of human nature."[72] His ethic was both personal and universal, and such a moral philosophy would not accept the sacrifice of anyone's value—even when those hoarding power overlooked

---

69 Mahan, *A Critical History of Philosophy*, Vol. 2, 230.
70 Mahan, "Certain Fundamental Principles, together with their Applications," 242.
71 Mahan, 242.
72 Mahan, *Autobiography: Intellectual, Moral, and Spiritual*, 169.

the intrinsic worth of others. Call him difficult. Call him stubborn. Call him inflexible. He was not going to be intimidated. Asa Mahan's childhood neighbors were absolutely correct. There was nothing halfway about him, and many without privilege were glad for this fact. He was an advocate and friend among those who often had no one else in their corner.

Five

A THEOLOGY FIT FOR JUSTICE

May We Trust Christ?

One of the nineteenth century's most significant religious movements might never have happened had it been born amid practices resembling today's academy. For the most part, our era considers scholarship a thing removed from student culture and questions. Those who write and publish leading ideas have career paths that limit their interaction with the raw insight of young people. To be an academic "success" means to gain ever-decreasing classroom responsibility and ever-increasing specialization. There are substantial exceptions. Thank goodness there are substantial exceptions.

Soon after Asa Mahan and Charles Finney settled in at Oberlin, a series of revival gatherings were held on campus in the fall of 1836. Mahan served as the preacher during most of these services. The major theme of this revival was Christian Perfection, Sanctification, or Holiness of heart and life—the way in which Christians respond to saving grace by living the love received from God.

A young man who had just graduated from the College's theological department, Sereno Wright Streeter, rose and asked his elders a critical question. According to Mahan's telling, the inquiry went as follows: "We are being instructed, and with undoubted correctness, that we are to trust Christ for sanctification just as we do for justification; and that we are to expect, and to receive, the one on the same condition on which we do the other. There is one question to which I desire to receive a definite answer,

137

namely, What *degree* of sanctification do the Scriptures authorise us to trust Christ for?"[1] The leaders of the school were floored. If they denied that such deliverance into full Christian maturity was possible, how were they different than any of those who taught that sin remained an unconquerable reality? If they affirmed the possibility of full sanctification, they could set a dangerous trend in motion. Mahan admitted later that he feared his students would rush into "perfectionism," a belief then circulating that claimed mature Christians were above God's law. All kinds of manipulative behavior and abuse came with this attitude.[2]

Therefore, Asa Mahan responded in the best way available to him. He withheld definitive judgment and promised to give the matter "prayerful and careful attention," hoping to offer a thoughtful answer in the future.[3] During that winter, when the College was in recess, Mahan accompanied Finney to the latter's church in New York City. At the "Broadway Tabernacle," the two devoted themselves to prayer and Bible study while formulating a credible answer to Streeter's haunting question.[4]

They also consulted John Wesley's *A Plain Account of Christian Perfection* and reached conclusions that were (at least in Mahan's case) remarkably akin to Methodist theology. Charles Finney spent the winter of 1836/1837 delivering a series of talks on Christian living. These were printed in *The New York Evangelist* and later collected for a book (1837).[5] The *Lectures to Professing Christians* included two chapters regarding "Christian Perfection." Because both Finney and Mahan agreed that Holiness or Christian Perfection entailed fulfillment of the law and not disregard for the law, they inevitably began with a definition of this very law.

---

1 Mahan, *Autobiography: Intellectual, Moral, and Spiritual*, 323. Sereno Wright Streeter is listed as having studied at Oberlin from 1834 to 1836. He was from Rowe, Massachusetts. See *Seventy-Fifth Anniversary General Catalogue of Oberlin College, 1833–1908* (Cleveland, Ohio: O. S. Hubbell Printing Co., 1909), 945.
2 Mahan, *Autobiography: Intellectual, Moral, and Spiritual*, 323–24.
3 Mahan, 324.
4 Warfield, *Studies in Perfectionism*, 54–55.
5 Warfield, 57.

Charles Finney's language came as no surprise: "The law of God requires perfect, disinterested, impartial benevolence, love to God and love to our neighbour."[6] His indebtedness to New England Theology was palpable. Even his preliminary considerations of Christian Perfection reflected the consequentialist theory of Samuel Hopkins—and less admirable teleological thinkers.

The second lecture on "Christian Perfection" addressed a matter Finney held in common with Mahan. According to the Oberlin professor, the primary reason why people do not receive full Christian maturity "is that they seek sanctification 'by works,' and not 'by Faith.'"[7] This became a familiar distinction throughout the movement. It was essentially a Wesleyan interpretation and guarded against the kind of legalism that seeks to earn one's way to Holiness. Thus the emphasis on fulfilling the moral law (not disregarding it) and the emphasis on keeping the moral law by grace avoided the twin dangers of antinomianism and legalism.

Asa Mahan had come upon this construction of sanctification before developing his more particular expression.[8] However, it was only after a good deal of study, prayer, and soul-searching that he presented his case for the doctrine of Christian Perfection. The critical moment arrived on the evening of Tuesday, September 4, 1838, when Mahan addressed the Oberlin "Society of Inquiry" regarding the question, "Is Perfection in Holiness Attainable in this Life?"[9] The presentation gained special recognition because it was published as the lead article in the inaugural issue of *The Oberlin Evangelist* (November 1, 1838). The *Evangelist* became a national-caliber vehicle for advancing the cause of Holiness or Christian Perfection, in addition to serving as a steadfast antislavery platform.

---

6   Charles G. Finney, *Lectures to Professing Christians*, 3rd ed. (London: Thomas Tegg, 1839), 215.

7   Finney, 230.

8   Asa Mahan, *Autobiography: Intellectual, Moral, and Spiritual*, 322–23.

9   Asa Mahan, "Is Perfection in Holiness Attainable in this Life?" *The Oberlin Evangelist* 1, no. 1 (November 1, 1838): 1–6.

Asa Mahan, like others, tended to approach the matter in two steps. First he defined the meaning of Christian Perfection. Then he devoted more lengthy analysis to the possibility of attaining such a state. His opening observations were not particularly unique. With regard to definition, Christian Perfection was "perfect obedience to the moral law. In other words, it is loving God with all our powers, and our neighbor as ourselves."[10] One might even presume that this was essentially the same thing claimed by Charles Finney. Yet in Mahan comments regarding the law of God were not filtered through language of "benevolence," disinterested or otherwise.

Mahan also qualified the meaning of perfection itself. For Oberlin's president, Christian Perfection did not imply perfect wisdom. Here he relied on a philosophical distinction that served him well during other scholarly conversations. The legitimately holy Christian might, as Mahan phrased things, live a perfection in kind that is finite in degree: "He is perfect in holiness whose love, at each successive moment, corresponds with the extent of his powers."[11] This was not a strategic scaling down of the sacred doctrine.

Mahan did not advocate a lightweight notion of Christian Perfection, but he did contend for a clear and credible one. Charles Finney may have expressed nascent ideas regarding Christian Perfection from Oberlin, but Asa Mahan set them in motion and gave them staying power. In 1839 Mahan released his 237-page *Scripture Doctrine of Christian Perfection*. Even the crusty Calvinist, B. B. Warfield, agreed that Mahan's book could be considered "the representative statement of the Oberlin Doctrine at this stage of its development."[12] Warfield tended to treat Finney as a wayward legalist bent on perpetuating the errors of New England. He was no more tolerant of Mahan's devotion to Christian Perfection, but he did acknowledge a difference between the two Oberlin leaders—a difference that appeared to paint Mahan in a slightly better light.

---

10 Mahan, 1.

11 Mahan, 1.

12 Warfield, *Studies in Perfectionism*, 64.

Overall, Warfield concluded that Asa Mahan's articulation of Christian Perfection echoed principles taught by John Wesley (something that was not necessarily the case with other Holiness champions).[13] Mahan said as much himself when he quoted Wesley. Christian Perfection was: "purity of intention, dedicating all the life to God. It is the giving God all the heart; it is one desire and design ruling all our tempers. It is devoting not a part, but all our soul, body and substance to God."[14] Of course, the definition of Holiness held its own disputed meanings, but it was the possibility or impossibility of reaching this maturity that seemed to generate the most controversy.

Because Asa Mahan placed Christian Perfection in the context of divine promises, he made the trustworthiness of God an issue. If Holiness was not a matter of human striving, then it became a matter of divine fulfillment. This put God on the hot seat. May we or may we not trust that God will deliver on the Holiness Mahan so fervently anticipated in this life? Such questions invited serious scrutiny and evoked much criticism aimed at Asa Mahan. Was he suggesting that people either embrace his theological argument or admit that they do not trust God? Many resented this supposed dilemma as a fabrication. Scores of written rebuttals to Mahan appeared in the church press. Some endorsed his work, but others saw it as a radical (and ill-advised) deviation from tradition. Yet those who knew Mahan best were probably not astonished that he stood at the center of debate.

The Hand that Fed Him

One constant throughout Asa Mahan's life was his positive relationships with students and former students. Those who clashed with him

---

13 Warfield, 67.

14 Asa Mahan, *Scripture Doctrine of Christian Perfection; With Other Kindred Subjects, Illustrated and Confirmed in A Series of Discourses Designed to Throw Light on the Way of Holiness* (Boston: D. S. King, 1839), 16–17. The quote is from Wesley's *A Plain Account of Christian Perfection*. See *The Works of John Wesley*, ed., Paul Wesley Chilcote and Kenneth J. Collins, Vol. 13, *Doctrinal and Controversial Treatises II* (Nashville: Abingdon Press, 2013), 190.

tended to be colleagues or elders defending institutionalized practices. The fact that Sereno Wright Streeter, a recent Oberlin graduate, entered into productive conversation with the president about the ways of Holiness fit a pattern. From early days when Mahan defended the "Lane Rebels" to his later years at Adrian College, students generally loved him. They did so not because he lacked eccentricities but because he remained real. They trusted that he loved them, respected them, and would not use them for professional advancement. This kind of rapport did not always exist between Asa Mahan and those who were once his professors.

A prominent example of friction appeared in Mahan's relationship with Andover's Leonard Woods. Woods (1774–1854) was born in Princeton, Massachusetts, and entered the Congregational ministry. He developed among the conflict between followers of Samuel Hopkins and the "old" Calvinists of more genteel persuasion. By the early nineteenth century, Woods had been instrumental in creating some union among these factions. His standing in both camps made him a logical choice to serve as the first professor of theology at Andover Seminary, founded during 1808. He held this pivotal position for thirty-eight years.[15]

The moderate Calvinism of Woods exhibited itself through meticulous critiques of Unitarianism at Harvard and the free-will proclivities advanced by Nathaniel William Taylor at Yale. Yet Woods tended to take less bombastic positions than the explicitly scholastic Calvinists at Princeton. Many experienced Leonard Woods as a rather understated and deliberate advocate for mainstream Calvinism.[16] Henry K. Rowe's 1933 *History of Andover Theological Seminary* recalled that Woods displayed "patience and sympathy with his friends and students."[17] Still, the adulatory narrative of Rowe admitted that, "Calvinism was a militant faith and

---

15 Dumas Malone, ed., *Dictionary of American Biography*, Vol. 20 (New York: Charles Scribner's Sons, 1943), 502.

16 Malone, 502.

17 Henry K. Rowe, *History of Andover Theological Seminary* (Boston: Thomas Todd Company, 1933), 49.

it bred theological warriors. Andover professors were expected to train their guns of orthodoxy against error, whether within or outside the walls of embattled Zion."[18] Leonard Woods seemed to dislike controversy, but his irenic nature did not prevent him from doing battle.

Asa Mahan entered Andover Seminary in 1824 and was graduated in 1827. Therefore, he studied with Woods while in his middle twenties—and while the professor was in his early fifties.[19] Mahan's 1839 *Scripture Doctrine of Christian Perfection* addressed many issues, but near the very end it looked back over the author's spiritual development. He recalled his earlier desire to grow in grace and the disappointments that followed. College did little to improve his maturity, and then he described his years at Andover:

> I subsequently entered a theological seminary, with the hope of there finding myself in such an atmosphere, that my first love would be revived. In this expectation, I grieve to say, I was most sadly disappointed. I found the piety of my brethren apparently as low as my own. I here say it with sorrow of heart, that my mind does not recur to a single individual connected with the "school of the prophets," when I was there, who appeared to me to enjoy daily communion and peace with God.[20]

Asa Mahan was describing Andover Seminary as led by Leonard Woods and others. His memory may have been more or less accurate, but his publication of this opinion fifteen years later was not exactly an act of diplomacy.

Woods responded at length to his former pupil through a series of articles, first published in the *American Biblical Repository* for January and April 1841. Not long after the essays were collected and released as a book: *An Examination of the Doctrine of Perfection, as held by Rev. Asa Mahan,*

---

18 Rowe, 49.

19 Madden and Hamilton, *Freedom and Grace: The Life of Asa Mahan*, 12–16.

20 Mahan, *Scripture Doctrine of Christian Perfection*, 225.

President of the Oberlin Collegiate Institute, Ohio, and Others (1841).[21] The writing of Woods was not a simple reaction to criticism by his former student. He held serious, theological reservations regarding Mahan's thesis, and he addressed the matter from an intellectual standpoint.

For starters, Woods suggested that Mahan overemphasized the difference between traditional Protestant theology and the Holiness teaching. He had no argument with the notion that *"full provision is made in the gospel, not only for the forgiveness of sin, but for the complete sanctification of God's people."*[22] However, this apparent agreement came with a catch. While Woods granted that entire sanctification was a core doctrine of his tradition, he denied that it was available during this life. What appeared to be a modest divide between Andover's sage and his former student was really a chasm. The overwhelming emphasis of Woods rejected any possibility of reaching a sanctified state in this world.

Leonard Woods did not make the distinction between "kind" and "degree" that grounded Mahan's thesis. Sanctification was viewed by him as an issue of either accomplishment or progression. There was no room for a both/and approach that Asa Mahan attempted to suggest. Faced with these opposing options, Woods maintained an impossibility of completion in this life and held out progression toward the goal as, in itself, an admirable spiritual quality. With reference to the notion that sanctification is God's law written on the heart, Woods countered: "Is it certain that the law cannot be written in the heart, *in some degree*, when it is not done perfectly?"[23] Mahan certainly employed the language of "degrees," but he and Woods meant something very different when they spoke in these terms. For Asa Mahan, degrees of growth were necessary, even

---

21 Leonard Woods, *An Examination of the Doctrine of Perfection, as held by Rev. Asa Mahan, President of the Oberlin Collegiate Institute, Ohio, and Others* (New York: W. R. Peters, 1841). The substance of these essays was published in *The Oberlin Evangelist* 3, no. 14 (July 7, 1841): 105–9, and 3, no. 15 (July 21, 1841): 113–19.

22 Woods, 15.

23 Woods, 31.

among those sanctified "in kind." Yet degrees of growth devoid of entire sanctification left something to be desired.

Very early in his essays, Woods suggested that Mahan fell into error through no want of Christian feeling but from "a hasty interpretation of Scripture, and a wrong method of reasoning."[24] This statement is especially intriguing given that the one Andover faculty member who seemed to leave a positive impression on Asa Mahan was biblical scholar Moses Stuart. Mahan credited Stuart with giving him a new understanding of Romans 7, a text traditionally used to assert the impossibility of entire sanctification. Many quoted the seemingly hopeless words: "For we know that the law is spiritual: but I am carnal, sold under sin" (KJV). However, Stuart approached the passage in a manner that challenged any sort of fatalism.

According to Moses Stuart, Paul's aim in Romans 7 was to contrast a legal and a proper Christian experience. In other words, the language of desperation did not reflect the apostle's conviction that sanctification is impossible—only that it is unattainable through works, human effort. This interpretation set Mahan's mind in motion regarding the possibility that one might be both justified *and* sanctified by grace through faith. The subsequent articulation of a Holiness theology was Mahan's doing, not something emphasized by Stuart, but the seed had been planted. In contrast, the theology of Leonard Woods seemed limited, indeed.[25]

Soon after the lengthy treatment by Woods was published, Mahan responded to the response (which is how these sorts of controversies tended to unfold). The August 4, 1841, issue of *The Oberlin Evangelist* featured a detailed reply by the Oberlin president. This essay is filled with point-by-point rebuttals, but it opens with a curious overarching argument. Mahan attempted to demonstrate polite regard for his former professor, but this decorum quickly shifted to strenuous objection: "The kind and Christian spirit which characterizes your recent review of my work on Christian Perfection is truly refreshing, and encourages me to address you in reply.

---

24 Woods, 11.

25 Mahan, *Out of Darkness into Light; or the Hidden Life Made Manifest*, 100–102.

You have unfortunately misapprehended my arguments, in almost every instance."[26] Mahan's major criticism emphasized a perceived "bait-and-switch" tactic by his opponents.

The Oberlin president sought to explore whether entire sanctification was possible in this life. He believed his detractors attempted to turn the debate toward an analysis of evidence regarding whether or not some have received this gift in the past. Mahan cared about both questions, but for him the first was of greatest importance.[27]

This framing of the debate reveals Asa Mahan's epistemological sensitivities. We ought to remember that the *Scripture Doctrine of Christian Perfection* (1839) was published very close to the release of his *Abstract of a Course of Lectures on Mental & Moral Philosophy* (1840). Near the beginning of the *Abstract*, Mahan explained the relationship between intuitive and experiential perceptions: "Experience, if it could give us what *is*, could not give us the fact that *what is, must be*."[28] Only intuitive perception can unlock universal and necessary truth. Inversely, an analysis of experience can only establish what has or has not happened in the past or the way things exist in the present. According to the president (and his Scottish influences) experience is very important, but there is more to knowing than experience. The future has its transcendental qualities and is an open book. This remained Asa Mahan's major point when he considered the possibility of entire sanctification.

It is probably not accurate to say that the Oberlin president bit the hand that had fed him in seminary. The contribution of Leonard Woods to Asa Mahan's growth remains unclear. However, Mahan's Holiness theology criticized his seminary training in a manner that might be considered bad form. One can admire his aim and advocacy for those without power and still acknowledge that he rubbed some establishment people the wrong way.

---

26 Asa Mahan, "Pres. Mahan's Reply to Dr. Woods," *The Oberlin Evangelist* 3, no. 16 (August 4, 1841): 121.

27 Mahan, 121.

28 Mahan, *Abstract of a Course of Lectures on Mental & Moral Philosophy*, 33.

Faculty Psychology and the Law of Love

Asa Mahan's intellectual versatility has been something of a problem for contemporary scholars. Those who focus on his role in the Holiness Movement rarely appreciate his command of Enlightenment-era philosophy. Those who examine his philosophical precision rarely place him within the context of Holiness theology. Such interpretive patterns say more about academic specialization than they do about Mahan's witness. Even his more explicitly theological views regarding sanctification were connected to established philosophical convictions.

Questions of sin and justification, forgiveness and growth in grace, demand an anthropology. What is human nature? What are our abilities and our proclivities to sin? How can redemption take place and healing practices be sustained? Borrowing from Enlightenment philosophical constructs, Asa Mahan employed a "faculty psychology" to explain these things. Accordingly, humans were posited as beings of three distinct faculties: the Intellect (or Intelligence), the Sensibility, and the Will.[29] He made explicit late in life the viewpoint he carried very early. His 1882 text, *The System of Mental Philosophy*, reiterated a fairly typical faculty psychology. Yet one curious fact dominated this book. Mahan is remembered for his emphasis on some freedom of the will. The *Mental Philosophy* devotes 185 pages to the Intellect, 74 to the Sensibility, and a mere 13 to the Will. [30]

This retrospective summation can be deceiving. Mahan's 1845 *Doctrine of the Will* was devoted exclusively to human agency, and it became a text celebrated for attempting to refute the Calvinistic determinism of Jonathan Edwards. The Oberlin president confronted many issues in this relatively short book, but careful readers will detect an impressively subtle and supple faculty psychology.

---

29 Discussion of Mahan's faculty psychology is drawn from: Christopher P. Momany, "Faculty Psychology in the Holiness Theology of Asa Mahan," *The Asbury Journal* 69, no. 2 (Fall 2014): 136–47.

30 Asa Mahan, *The System of Mental Philosophy* (Chicago: S. C. Griggs and Company, 1882).

Mahan granted that the Intellect and Sensibility are dominated by involuntary characteristics. We know that which we know and feel that which we feel, but the universe of action has a quality all its own. We are not destined to act in the way that we know or feel things.[31] Asa Mahan's description of this peculiar freedom may invite debate today. Traditional Wesleyans might wonder whether the president stressed an independent or a graciously restored kind of freedom. Yet the way Mahan placed his philosophical anthropology within a theology that stressed both justification and sanctification by grace mattered. Where grace abounds, it is difficult to write off the appreciation for freedom as some stubbornly independent or prideful reliance on the self.

The eleventh chapter of the *Doctrine of the Will* is crucial. Here Mahan addressed the relationship between the Intellect, the Sensibility, and the Will when action is deemed morally right and when it is deemed morally wrong. His language is revealing: "In all acts and states morally right, the Will is in harmony with the Intelligence, from respect to moral obligation or duty; and all the desires and propensities, all the impulses of the Sensibility, are held in strict subordination. In all acts morally wrong, the Will is controlled by the Sensibility, irrespective of the dictates of the Intelligence."[32] This statement may lead one to conclude that Mahan was suspicious of all feeling, that he was some kind of cold formalist. However, the real key to these remarks is the Intelligence.

Consistent with his primal regard for realism, Mahan trusted humanity's ability to know the world outside, its character, and especially its value. In fact, his focus on the Intellect, as opposed to the Sensibility, expressed Mahan's way of avoiding self-absorption. His brand of realism, bolstered by Kantian deontology, was not so much an overconfident theory of knowledge as it was a reminder that we have obligations to those around us, even when we do not *feel* such commitment.

This other-directedness was given more specific articulation when Mahan moved into a discussion of the moral law. As with his *Abstract*

---

31 Asa Mahan, *Doctrine of the Will* (New York: Mark H. Newman, 1845), 124–29.
32 Mahan, 156.

and Moral Philosophy, the *Doctrine of the Will* emphasized the "intrinsic worth" of people. Perhaps most powerful is a passage in Mahan's book on the Will that seems to have been drawn directly from his handwritten manuscript. The notes state:

> Fundamental characteristic of right intention or what does the moral law really require.
>
> 1st. Statement All objects known to us esteemed according to their intrinsic worth. From this results the two precepts of law Love to God—& to man.
>
> 2nd. Kant's statement. So will an intent, that you may properly regard the motive from which you act as a rule to all intelligents.
>
> 3 Cousin's The impossibility of not erecting the motive, when it is right, into a universal rule
>
> Remarks 1. These identical
>
> 2. This conformed to the bible
>
> 3. These present the nature of the *law* as required in the bible[33]

In the *Doctrine of the Will*, Mahan also followed his focus on the intrinsic worth of persons with references to Immanuel Kant and Victor Cousin:

> The same principle has been announced in a form somewhat different by Kant, to wit: "So act that thy maxim of Will (intention) might become law in a system of universal moral obligation"— that is, let your controlling intention be always such, that all Intelligents may properly be required ever to be under the supreme control of the same intention.
>
> By Cousin, the same principle is thus announced: "The moral principle being universal, the sign, the external type by which a resolution may be recognized as conformed to this principle,

---

33 Asa Mahan, "Manuscript Writings, Miscellaneous," Archives, Shipman Library, Adrian College, page 106.

is the impossibility of not erecting the immediate motive (intention) of the particular act or resolution, into a maxim of universal legislation"—that is, we cannot but affirm that every moral agent in existence is bound to act from the same motive or intention.[34]

This exceedingly close philosophical reasoning may seem miles removed from Asa Mahan's Holiness theology, but it was critical to his understanding of sanctification.

The very first chapter of the *Scripture Doctrine of Christian Perfection* links Mahan's definition of Holiness to a healthy interaction of the mental faculties. Within the sanctified person, the intellectual powers will seek "the truth and will of God, and by what means we may best meet the demands of the great law of love."[35] Likewise, the feelings and susceptibilities will be "in perfect and perpetual harmony with the truth and will of God as apprehended by the intellect."[36] The actions of a sanctified person will be "in entire conformity to the will of God."[37] Therefore, Holiness could be described as seeing reality the way God sees it and acting in conformity with this vision.

An even more detailed explication of the role faculty psychology played in Asa Mahan's Holiness teaching can be found among his manuscript notebook. Here he pondered in considerable detail the implications of the faculties for sanctification. Underscoring these notes is a connection between the conception of Christian perfection and that of "truth." Mahan referenced John 17:17: "Sanctify them through thy truth."[38] Whether Mahan's interpretation of "truth" was the same thing intended by the writer of the Fourth Gospel can be argued. Yet truth, in some capacity, anchored the Oberlin president's approach to Holiness, just as it figured prominently in his faculty psychology.

---

34 Mahan, *Doctrine of the Will*, 164.

35 Mahan, *Scripture Doctrine of Christian Perfection*, 14.

36 Mahan, 15.

37 Mahan, 13.

38 Asa Mahan, "Manuscript Writings, Miscellaneous," Archives, Shipman Library, Adrian College, Page 65.

A considerable part of Mahan's emphasis on truth can be traced to his belief in a knowable, objective reality. These same notes on sanctification stress that the holy person is one whose intention "will be in perfect harmony with the nature, character, and relations of all objects apprehended by the intelligence."[39] Moreover, one's "feelings will correspond with the nature of the objects presented."[40] The interaction between Asa Mahan's faculty psychology and his theology of Holiness was so complete that it is virtually impossible to extricate one from the other.

While some might question the role played by the Sensibility in Mahan's Holiness teaching, others may find his focus on realities outside of the self to be refreshing. There is nothing in his witness that deprecates properly ordered affections, but there is plenty in his thought to prevent the tradition from turning into incessant navel-gazing. This is perhaps one of Asa Mahan's most enduring contributions. Holiness was not conceived as a private purity. It was considered an honest posture of love. Recognition of the value presented by things and people (and a distinction between the two) grounded his theology. In turn, this perspective nurtured a principled concern for justice. Rarely was such a description of the interior life linked so directly to clear and authentic relationships with the world and its people.

Three Models of Atonement

Asa Mahan exuded many eccentricities. Among them was his rather confusing method of note-taking. Mahan's handwritten manuscript of lecture outlines and sermon material reflects the nonlinear development of his thinking. He often began rather precise outlines, continued for several pages, and then abruptly changed topics. The new topic would be pursued for three or four pages before returning to the former subject, at which point he finished his original outline. This pattern surrounded his writing

---

39 Mahan, 66.
40 Mahan, 66.

about sanctification. The notes on Holiness were wrapped in a detailed discussion regarding the doctrine of atonement.

This juxtaposition of atonement and sanctification raises many questions. One topic addresses God's saving action in history; the other, humanity's growth in grace. They are not at all mutually exclusive, but their entanglement throughout Mahan's notebook may seem odd. It is probably not an intentional pairing. Yet their shared location in this text demonstrates the way Oberlin's president held much together in his mind at the same time.

Mahan's treatment of the atonement resembles his analysis of other doctrines. He broke the topic down through basic distinctions: in this case the "nature" and the "extent" of the atonement. The latter category moved him to make bold and unique claims regarding the expanse of God's love, but the former reflected a rather traditional Protestant theology. Early in the manuscript, well before the twin discussion of atonement and sanctification, Mahan asked: "Has an atonement actually been made for the sin of transgressors?"[41] He established, to the approval of his mind, that there existed a deep need for atonement and a remedy for humanity's plight. He wrote that the atonement is "the substitution of the sufferings and death of Christ in the place of the eternal punishment of sinners."[42] Such language may not strike the reader as being all that unusual, but it does reveal much about Mahan's theology.

Since the origin of Christianity, thinkers and writers have posited several theories regarding the atonement. The manner in which Jesus's death expressed victory over evil or the manner in which his death satisfied a need for judgment, as well as other considerations, have dominated this reflection. After the Protestant Reformation many adopted a view that Christ's death freed humanity from futile attempts to keep God's law through effort and performance. Jesus stood in the gap, took our place, paid the price for sin, and opened a new way. It is not incidental that Asa Mahan employed the language of "substitution" when speaking of the

41 Mahan, 17.
42 Mahan, 60.

atonement. He meant exactly that—God in Christ served as a substitute for us when it came time to square the ledger. Today's Christian may argue the merits or flaws within this theology, but a careful reading of Mahan's notebook makes plain that substitution remained critical for him.

The substitutionary motif may not seem any different from the doctrinal convictions of most mid-nineteenth-century Protestant pastors. Yet, once again, the totality of Mahan's thinking presents several complexities. Those who study various atonement theories often credit (or blame) Enlightenment philosophers for giving new energy to a "moral influence" approach. This school of thought did not originate in the eighteenth century, but since that time many have linked it with modern thinkers (even Immanuel Kant). According to this interpretation, Enlightenment sages denied the substitutionary necessity of Jesus's death. Instead, the life, death, and resurrection of Jesus serve as a profound example for moral change—an inspiration to live a different kind of life—a catalyst for ethical renewal. Kant often gets categorized as a proponent of the moral influence approach, but he criticized this view, along with the others.[43]

There were many things about Immanuel Kant's thought that Asa Mahan admired, but the disregard for Jesus's atonement was not one of them. A carefully constructed integration of evangelical Protestant theology and critical philosophy set the Oberlin president apart from most college professors and presidents. However, Mahan's articulation became especially provocative when it shifted from considering the "nature" of the atonement and explored the "extent" of the atonement.

According to his autobiography, Mahan grappled very early in life with several theories of atonement. He stated that "the system of doctrine in which I was educated took three distinct and antagonistic forms: the old school or limited atonement and natural inability theory, the Hopkinsian or general atonement and natural ability theory, and the Divine efficiency

---

43 There is more to this conversation than meets the eye. See for example Drayton C. Benner, "Immanuel Kant's Demythologization of Christian Theories of Atonement in *Religion within the Limits of Reason Alone*," *Evangelical Quarterly* 79, no. 2 (2007): 99–111.

theory, the theory of Dr. Emmons."[44] The first was the standard Calvinist theory that Jesus died for the elect, and humanity possessed no natural ability to turn from wrong and choose the right. The second was a variation on the first approach but differed in one important regard. This view claimed that Jesus died for all in general. Thus humanity had a *natural* ability to do right but inevitably failed because of a *moral* inability. The third accepted this distinction between natural and moral ability but argued that God works directly to drive human behavior, good or bad. Young Asa Mahan settled on the third theory as a sort of stopgap position. Yet he would change as the years unfolded.

When Mahan addressed the "extent" of the atonement in his personal notebook, he began by proclaiming that, "It is designed for every individual of the race."[45] This language, though comprehensive, can be read in several ways. Near this claim is another statement that the atonement is "universal in its extent."[46] Mahan referenced 1 John 2:2, John 3:16-17, and Hebrews 2:9. Still, it is unclear whether he was describing a general atonement and natural ability that lacked moral ability or a universal atonement that led to universalism (the doctrine that all are eventually saved). As it turned out, he advocated neither of these positions. Mahan's view was certainly comprehensive, even exhaustive, but it did not champion universalism.

Discourse VI of the *Christian Perfection* came closest to clarifying his position. Here he presented a variation on the threefold consideration of atonement. In this context, the first was the limited atonement of standard Calvinism. The second captured the theories of general atonement. Mahan said nothing here about natural and moral ability. The third and preferred view he called "special atonement." This last took the notion of general atonement further and invoked the language of Hebrews 2:9: "Christ, instead of dying for no one in particular, died for *every man in*

---

44 Mahan, *Autobiography: Intellectual, Moral, and Spiritual*, 110.

45 Asa Mahan, "Manuscript Writings, Miscellaneous," Archives, Shipman Library, Adrian College, page 70.

46 Mahan, 70.

particular."[47] The painful and painstaking sacrifice for each and all did not automatically end in universalism. God's astoundingly particular and universal love summoned "the reception of grace by the sinner."[48] This was consistent with Mahan's move away from divine efficiency theories and toward an emphasis on human agency. He maintained that even the stunning sacrifice of God in Jesus Christ for each and every person remained open to reception or rejection.

It would be easy to dismiss this finely ground comparison of atonement theories. Contemporary church cultures often consider these debates arcane and irrelevant. They are not. Conversations about the atonement may appear to be unnecessary nit-picking, but they reveal assumptions about the nature of humanity and the meaning of redemption. Professional theologians often treat such questions as opportunities to score points at academic conferences, and leaders in the church often write them off as theoretical wastes of time. They are neither.

How one conceives of human brokenness and the means of reclamation is critical. I have argued elsewhere that some sort of traditional atonement theory is absolutely necessary for justice. A God who was not in Christ makes the sacrifice of Jesus abusive. Only a God who participates fully in our pain and failure can redeem. Likewise, a God who came as Jesus for select human beings implies that some do not matter. A God who came— lived, died, and rose—for each and all makes a tremendous statement of value.[49] When this unconditional initiative of God is coupled with a carefully construed understanding of human agency, love and justice reign.

This was precisely the case with the theology of Asa Mahan. We can almost sense his deontological ethical theory when he speaks of Jesus coming for each and every person in particular. His is no view of the atonement that calculates who may be worthy of saving and who may need to perish for a perceived greater good. Grace is God's prerogative, and according to

---

47 Mahan, *Scripture Doctrine of Christian Perfection*, 153–54.
48 Mahan, 154.
49 Christopher P. Momany, "In Defense of Atonement Theology: Affirmation of Being," *The Christian Century*, February 5, 2014, 25–27.

the Oberlin president, it is available for every individual. Some might consider this an individualism, a catering to every voice against the common good. Yet in Mahan's day (as in our own) this complaint typically came from the powerful who found it inconvenient to value those without clout. Agree with him or disagree. Asa Mahan was consistent. Moral theories that sacrificed some for the agendas of others were wrong, as were theories of the atonement that failed to acknowledge God's love for each and every human being. There was a certain elegance among his traditional views. They did not reflect Immanuel Kant's approach to the atonement, but Mahan's theology led to principles reminiscent of Kant's ethic.

The Evangelical Spirit

According to Asa Mahan, there was no such thing as "Oberlin Perfectionism," at least when the doctrine of Holiness found proper expression. Generations of observers, scholars, and commentators (not the least being B. B. Warfield) applied the term "perfectionism" to many views, even the theology of Holiness propagated by Mahan. The Oberlin president insisted that there was an insurmountable difference between his teaching and that which might be called "perfectionism." Perfectionism referred to an aberrant phenomenon that disregarded the moral law. Scriptural Holiness or Christian perfection held the moral law in exceedingly high regard. As Mahan put it: "The doctrine of holiness, now under consideration, in all its essential features and elements, stands in direct opposition to Perfectionism. It has absolutely nothing in common with it, but a few terms derived from the Bible."[50] Moreover, according to Mahan, the few terms invoked by perfectionists did not make their theology biblical.

Under this general repudiation of perfectionism, Mahan included a more detailed, eight-point indictment. The first spoke volumes: "Perfectionism, for example, in its fundamental principles, is the abrogation of all law. The doctrine of holiness, as here maintained, is perfect obedience to the precepts of the law. It is the 'righteousness of the law fulfilled in

---

50 Mahan, *Scripture Doctrine of Christian Perfection*, 86.

us.' "[51] The biblical reference was drawn from Romans 8:4 and echoed the significance Romans 7 and 8 held in Mahan's Holiness theology.

There were many reasons for Asa Mahan's sharp distinction between an articulation of Holiness and views known as perfectionism. For one, he was responding to currents of the time. Just as Mahan developed his theology an alternative trend arose in New England and parts of New York State. This type of perfectionism boasted many advocates but none better known than John Humphrey Noyes (1811–1886). Noyes was born in Brattleboro, Vermont, and educated at Dartmouth College. Like Asa Mahan, Noyes studied for a period among Andover Seminary but transferred to the Theological Department at Yale. He embraced Yale's reaction to traditional Calvinist ideas and announced in February 1834 that he had attained a state of perfection. The declaration did not go unnoticed, and Noyes was ostracized by college and church authorities. Eventually he became the leader of several utopian communities.[52]

One of the most controversial ideas taught by Noyes held that "monogamic marriage" was incompatible with perfectionism. In other words, he espoused support for "open" marriage or free love.[53] This teaching was guaranteed to create a storm of criticism and reflected the general disregard for moral law among perfectionists. We cannot be certain that Mahan had Noyes in mind when he wrote his 1839 *Scripture Doctrine of Christian Perfection*, but there is evidence that this was the case. The sixth rebuttal offered by the Oberlin president charged that, "Perfectionism abrogates the Sabbath, and all the ordinances of the gospel, and, in its legitimate tendencies, even marriage itself."[54] In sum, Mahan believed that perfectionism was really "the perfection of licentiousness," and one who revered the moral law could never travel this road.[55]

---

51 Mahan, 86.

52 Dumas Malone, ed., *Dictionary of American Biography*, Vol. 13 (New York: Charles Scribner's Sons, 1943), 589–90.

53 Malone, 589.

54 Mahan, *Scripture Doctrine of Christian Perfection*, 87–88, 214–16.

55 Mahan, 88.

The inevitable conflict over God's law guided Asa Mahan's critique, but just as important was the way perfectionists attempted to justify their neglect of the law. According to Mahan, a misunderstanding of the Holy Spirit made disregard of the law possible. Perfectionists, the president claimed, taught that "the Spirit now communicates truth to Christians by direct revelation, and hence the study of the Scriptures, the ministry of reconciliation, prayer, the Sabbath, and all the ordinances, and the church itself, they wholly dispensed with."[56] In 1870 Asa Mahan would publish his own controversial book on the person and work of the Holy Spirit (*The Baptism of the Holy Ghost*), but he never invoked the Spirit as an excuse for neglecting the moral law.

Perfectionists seemed to substitute "impressions and impulses" for the proper teachings of the Spirit.[57] This error led to "maintaining that every existing desire or impulse is produced by the direct agency of the Spirit, and therefore to be gratified."[58] For one whose faculty psychology kept a tight rein on the Sensibility and its often-questionable impulses, the perfectionist logic was unacceptable. Mahan agreed that the Holy Spirit communicated truth, but it was a truth confirmed by the Intelligence— and consistent with Scripture. These may appear to be delicate distinctions, but they addressed absolutely fundamental differences in theology.

The alternative promoted by Asa Mahan went beyond criticism of perfectionism and affirmation of the law. He sought to situate the debate in a threefold analysis. Drawing on his personal experience with notions such as justification and sanctification, Mahan argued that there were really three interpretations available to Christians. First, there was the antinomian view. This antipathy for the law (*nomos*) resembled the teaching and practice of perfectionists. As described by the Oberlin president: "The Antinomian spirit relies upon Christ for *justification*, in the absence of personal holiness, or sanctification. It looks to him to be saved *in* but not

---

56 Mahan, 215.
57 Mahan, 215.
58 Mahan, 215.

from sin."[59] Mahan saw this as an artificial reception of grace, an appropriation of freedom without subsequent change.

The second interpretive lens was that of the legal spirit. This, Mahan claimed, could appear in two forms. First, it might attempt to achieve justification and sanctification through effort or human deeds. Second, it might embrace some form of justification by grace and then seek sanctification through effort to keep the law. Asa Mahan's earlier experience resembled this second type of legalism. He awakened to the gift of grace as a young person but then struggled to grow through dint of resolution and determination. By 1839 he had observed that the spiritual exhaustion of such a life guaranteed tragic resignation.[60]

Therefore, Mahan articulated and advocated a third approach, that of "the evangelical spirit."[61] The evangelical spirit was not a collection of doctrines, and it was certainly not a cultural or political viewpoint. It was reliance upon grace for both the forgiveness found in justification and the mature practices of sanctification. As expressed by Mahan, "The evangelical spirit looks to Christ alike for justification and sanctification both, and, by implicit faith in him, obtains a blissful victory over the 'world, the flesh, and the devil.'"[62] The law of God was neither unimportant nor something to be met through tireless effort. The law of God was a way of Holiness empowered by grace.

Mahan's understanding of the evangelical spirit gave his theology a Wesleyan character lacking in many who came from Presbyterian or Congregational backgrounds. He did not accept Calvinist views regarding natural or moral inability, and he avoided simplistic theories of the will's freedom that others expounded. He is not often given credit for possessing

---

59 Mahan, 121.

60 Mahan, 121–22.

61 Mahan, 122.

62 Mahan, 122. A later exploration of the antinomian, legal, and evangelical spirits is found in Asa Mahan, *Life Thoughts on the Rest of Faith* (London: F. E. Longley, 1877), 57–61.

a more nuanced approach to the will because his 1845 book (*Doctrine of the Will*) was so unequivocal. He stood firmly on the side of freedom.

Yet the freedom of the will embraced by Asa Mahan was something that he later termed a dependent freedom. His autobiography recalled the great western revivals of 1824 to 1832 and attributed much of the movement's success to a belief in "the absolute freedom of the human will."[63] People were not predestined to some fate. They could choose to receive or reject the gospel, but Mahan found modest fault with this new doctrine: "It had in it, as half-truths always have, the elements of fatal error."[64] He continued: "We are free agents: but the freedom which we and all creatures possess is a dependent one. Of us it will remain eternally true, that 'we are not sufficient of ourselves to think' (much less do) 'any thing as of ourselves: but our sufficiency is of God.' "[65] Drawing on 2 Corinthians 3:5 Mahan underscored his major point: teaching the doctrine of ability "as an absolute and not dependent power" leads to pride of self-sufficiency.[66] There was so much more to the gospel.

At the root of things, Asa Mahan was a theologian of relationships. Both antinomianism and legalism ended in stubborn, deathly isolation. Those who disregard the law go it alone. Those who try to fulfill the law on their own terms will fail. Only those who live in relationship with God know grace. A direct and necessary relationship with God in Jesus Christ allows one to live freely for others. The evangelical spirit was both intensely personal and unconditionally social. God's comprehensive love burned as an all-consuming fire.

The Perils of Prophecy

It is impossible to comprehend the entirety of Asa Mahan's tenure at Oberlin. He certainly did not spend all of his time teaching and writing books about philosophy and theology. However, given the administrative and

---

63 Mahan, *Autobiography: Intellectual, Moral, and Spiritual*, 244.
64 Mahan, 244.
65 Mahan, 244.
66 Mahan, 244.

pastoral responsibilities he bore, it is somewhat mind-boggling to consider his prolific publication record. Today many scholars perfect the art of avoiding as many administrative duties as possible, and administrators are (with notable exceptions) rarely scholars. Mahan was both. We might presume that it was easier to integrate the two vocations in his age, but that would be a self-serving assumption. Asa Mahan was not the only scholar/administrator to cross boundaries, not even at Oberlin. There were many sturdy souls who took intellectual engagement seriously, even as they sought to help order communities.

Mahan was involved in practical movements of the day as well. Variously, he participated in dietary and health improvement programs, the manual labor approach to higher education, and curricular reform—along with both the women's rights and antislavery causes. He even lent his stature to many of the international peace conferences that developed before the Civil War. The Oberlin president was not a retiring person. Engagement was his trademark, and along with engagement came a sharp articulation of views.

The Oberlin Collegiate Institute, like most communities, was never quite as tranquil and united as advertised. By 1844 Mahan's abrupt manner of relating to the faculty led to a call for his resignation. Letters of critique and support regarding his personality and leadership style were exchanged until an uneasy truce was formed. The reconciliation did not hold much promise. There were subsequent disagreements over faculty salaries, and Mahan's advocacy for the women of the Institute put him at odds with many professors.[67] Twentieth- and twenty-first-century scholarship has tended to view this conflict through the typical lens of faculty/administration struggle. Yet here the matter was more complex.

The faculty at Oberlin had unusual power for its day. Negotiations that brought Mahan, Finney, and many of the Lane students to town included provision for wider faculty prerogative regarding admission to the school,

---

67 Madden and Hamilton, *Freedom and Grace: The Life of Asa Mahan*, 99–126. Madden and Hamilton offer an incredibly detailed chronology of Mahan's conflict with the faculty and trustees.

overseeing the curriculum, and hiring of professors. On February 10, 1835, "The Trustees committed to the Faculty the internal management of the institution; 'provided always, that the Faculty be holden amenable to the Board of Trustees, and not liable to censure of interruption from the Board so long as their measures shall not infringe on the laws or general principles of the institution.' "[68] This policy created an environment where the faculty had more administrative authority, even as the president contributed to academic life.

During the winter of 1849/1850, Asa Mahan traveled to England. While lecturing there, the Oberlin faculty renewed their campaign to have him removed from the presidency. Upon his return to the college, Mahan assessed the actions against him and asked for an official statement from the faculty. They obliged. Over the course of the next month, letters for and against the president circulated. A special meeting of the trustees was called for April 18, 1850, and a list of grievances was prepared by the faculty. After revision, the document was accepted by the entire faculty and included a ten-point complaint.[69]

Leading the list was a general criticism. The president, it read, "should see that his self-esteem has amounted to self-conceit and has led him to overrate both his natural abilities and his moral attainments, and that under the same influence he underrates the ability and character of his brethren."[70] One is hard-pressed to understand why the language of natural ability and moral attainment appears in the document. Since these two categories were so important among Oberlin discussions of Holiness, there might be more to the charge than is apparent. At the least, the faculty experienced Mahan as a harsh brother, one whose exacting standards of spiritual life pinched.

---

68 *Seventy-Fifth Anniversary General Catalogue of Oberlin College, 1833–1908*, 38.
69 Madden and Hamilton, *Freedom and Grace: The Life of Asa Mahan*, 105–9.
70 Treasurer's Records, Misc., Archives, Oberlin College, Asa Mahan Folder, Box 8.

The criticism was based in fact. Beyond personal interactions, Mahan published a sermon in *The Oberlin Evangelist* titled, "The Lukewarm Professor."[71] By "professor" he meant simply anyone professing to follow Christ, but the indictment probably riled his professional colleagues more than others. The Oberlin president drew from Revelation 3:15-16: "I know thy works, that thou art neither cold nor hot: I would thou wert cold or hot. So then, because thou art lukewarm, and neither cold nor hot, I will spue thee out of my mouth (KJV)." This text is often employed to blast those with insufficient zeal, but close reading reminds us that the Revelation played a pivotal role in Mahan's ethic.

The sermon's opening observes that judgment comes as the Son of God "walks in terror amid the golden candlesticks."[72] This reference to the Revelation's often-confusing imagery would go unnoticed—except that Mahan returned to the language of "golden candlesticks" later in life, when writing his commentary on the United States Constitution. The substance of his criticism charged that many who profess to follow Jesus do so in form but not in power. They adhere to basic societal conventions associated with the faith but fail to live the whole gospel. They trust past experience of conviction and redemption instead of ongoing intimacy with God.

The reference to experience is especially intriguing. Mahan believed that the lukewarm relied on *past experience* as the ground of hope."[73] They tended to "dwell much on past experience, with nothing new at the present time."[74] While this critique certainly followed a common pattern by stressing the need for a living relationship with Christ, it also reflected Mahan's epistemological sensitivities. He was, after all, one who valued experience as an indicator of truth, while also holding that experience could not determine what must be true. His qualified respect for

---

71 Asa Mahan, "The Lukewarm Professor," *The Oberlin Evangelist* 9, no. 26 (December 22, 1847): 201–3.

72 Mahan, 201.

73 Mahan, 202.

74 Mahan, 202.

experience did not only point to the importance of transcendent, necessary truths. It also pointed toward God's future. He even tossed in a charge that reflected his faculty psychology: the lukewarm possessed affections that were moved more "by things seen than by things unseen."[75] The transcendent and unconditional must be embraced now, with the hope that it will become a reality in God's time.

Charles Finney's involvement in the controversy remains somewhat clouded to this day. It appears that, by the end of the drama, he was on the side of the faculty. Edward Madden and James Hamilton concluded that, "Finney was a cautious person and committed to the greatest happiness principle and was bound to find Mahan unpalatable. Finney never wholeheartedly embraced any reform except the regeneration of souls through revivals."[76] This application of Finney's consequentialist theory is perhaps overstated, but it does throw light on his behavior.

In any case, Mahan's searing judgment of lukewarm people did not sit well with his colleagues, and over the years the conflict of 1849/1850 has received many interpretations. According to Robert Fletcher's two-volume history of Oberlin College (1943), the mess was almost entirely driven by Mahan's dictatorial personality.[77] By the 1980s Madden and Hamilton pushed back and argued that the conflict revolved around Mahan's admirable (though acerbic) commitment to reform.[78]

During an address given in 1984, noted historian Geoffrey Blodgett had this to say about the contrasting interpretations: "I think they are both right—that Mahan's behavior was blunt and tactless precisely because his commitments were so unguarded and intense."[79] Then Blodgett added an observation: "Mahan's positions in succeeding quarrels were more often

---

75 Mahan, 202.

76 Madden and Hamilton, *Freedom and Grace: The Life of Asa Mahan*, 118–19.

77 Robert Samuel Fletcher, *A History of Oberlin College: From Its Foundation through the Civil War*, 2 vols. (Oberlin, Ohio: Oberlin College, 1943).

78 Madden and Hamilton, *Freedom and Grace: The Life of Asa Mahan*, 116–26.

79 Geoffrey Blodgett, "Reformist Zeal Gets Mahan to Oberlin Presidency—then Costs Him the Job," *Contact: Adrian College Bulletin* (Winter 1984): 7.

than not more advanced and forward-looking than those of his Oberlin critics. Time and again he was out in front."[80] While Blodgett may not have intended this language to be so eschatological (concerned with God's coming kingdom), he certainly hit a vein that ran deep in both Mahan's ethical theory and theology.

Today we often use the term "prophetic" to speak of social justice, and we often use the term "prophecy" to speak of prediction or anticipation regarding God's reign. Those on the left tend to prefer the former language, those on the right the latter. For Asa Mahan the terms and their respective meanings belonged together. This is but one of many reasons why his life remains so provocative.

In spite of his open conflict and stern demeanor with professional colleagues, Mahan maintained a genuine, egalitarian set of relationships with those outside established power. For instance, one of the faculty charges against Mahan read thus: "He should refrain from agitating the minds of the Students on questions which involve the established order of the institution."[81] This is not a typical complaint raised by college faculties against a president. Honesty requires an admission: most contemporary faculty/administration conflicts invoke the best interest of students. In reality, students inevitably pay a price for lacking real power among the threefold relationship. The Oberlin controversy was different. Here the faculty stated that the president was somehow a subversive influence among the student body!

Perhaps most notable is a petition of support for Asa Mahan offered by eighty-six African American residents of the wider Oberlin community: "We have long looked upon you as being among our firmest and most able friends."[82] Among the signatures was that of John Copeland, a man who would later participate in the Oberlin-Wellington rescue and who would eventually die in John Brown's failed 1859 raid at Harpers Ferry.[83]

---

80 Blodgett, 7.
81 Treasurer's Records, Misc., Archives, Oberlin College, Asa Mahan Folder, Box 8.
82 Treasurer's Records, Misc., Archives, Box 8.
83 Madden and Hamilton, *Freedom and Grace: The Life of Asa Mahan*, 108.

In August of 1850 Asa Mahan tendered his resignation. He was already working on a new endeavor in Cleveland, but in fact he had been pushed out of Oberlin. The degree to which Mahan's fate was self-inflicted can be argued. Often neglected in the analysis is the way he kept his eyes on the horizon, a horizon that others disputed and denied—and that he could only see dimly. Yet he did strain for the world God intended.

Six

THE REALM OF ENDS
AND A NATION WITHOUT END

The Road to Adrian

Eighteen hundred and fifty was a year of upheaval throughout the United States. While Asa Mahan and colleagues were engaged in localized animosity, the whole country was in crisis over the issue of slavery. Several decades of avoidance and appeasement could no longer hold. The drive for westward expansion intensified sectional rivalries. The rush to California and the likelihood that this region would enter the Union as a free state—among other matters—created unbearable pressure. Those in Washington concluded that some grand "compromise" was needed to keep the whole country from blowing apart.

By January of 1850 Henry Clay, Daniel Webster, and other players began to strategize. They would cobble together one great bill or a series of bills to placate the South without creating terminal alienation throughout the North. The whole story is complex and full of patchwork dealmaking that would cause most honorable souls to blush. The end result was called "The Compromise of 1850."

A shorthand description of the Compromise goes something like this: the Fugitive Slave Act of 1793 was made more stringent. The slave trade in Washington, DC, was ended. California did in fact enter the Union as a free state, while a territorial government was established in Utah. The Compromise also settled a boundary dispute between Texas and New

Mexico and addressed the debt that Texas brought into the Union. During the process, a territorial government was created in New Mexico.[1]

The term "compromise" is a fickle beast. To those enfranchised the result may have fit the language, but for several million "compromise" was simply a perfecting of their already desperate fate. Perhaps the most incendiary part of the whole package was the strengthening of the "Fugitive Slave" legislation. Southerners argued that this was only a clarification of Article IV, Section 2, of the United States Constitution, but antislavery folk were not convinced. Moreover, the new law had the effect of nationalizing interests previously tolerated within certain states. Federal officials were enlisted to issue warrants for the return of people seeking freedom on the Underground Railroad, and there were penalties for those in the north who would not aid in capturing so-called "fugitives." Additionally, federally appointed commissioners were paid $10 if they rendered a decision in favor of "owners." They were paid $5 if they found in favor of people seeking freedom.[2]

The whole legal landscape dripped with irony. Those invested in perpetuating slavery lived and breathed the grammar of "states' rights," but they had no problem wielding federal power for their special interest. Those who believed the federal government possessed a right to end or at least to restrict slavery found they had been drafted to defend the system.

The Compromise of 1850 became law in September of that year, but the heated moments of debate unfolded during the previous winter and spring. In fact, at precisely the same time Asa Mahan traded accusations with his colleagues in Oberlin, speeches of monumental importance thundered throughout Congress. Daniel Webster delivered his oration in favor of the Compromise on March 7, 1850, and William Henry Seward spoke against the legislation on March 11. Seward, perhaps unwittingly,

---

1   An insightful and accessible treatment of the Compromise can be found in Michael S. Green, *Politics and America in Crisis: The Coming of the Civil War* (Santa Barbara, California: Praeger, 2010), 19–43.

2   Green, 50.

set the capitol ablaze with his language regarding a "higher law" than the Constitution.[3]

This context might lead us to charge Oberlin with petty bickering while the nation stood at the abyss, but that would be a rather harsh judgment. The orators in Washington sported great name recognition, but their maneuvering was no more inspiring than anything taking place among smaller communities. Even Seward, the great saint of the higher law, turned out to be less consistent than his speech suggested. Those in Oberlin and in a thousand other places made their own contributions for the good or ill of humanity.

As for Asa Mahan, he began the turbulent 1850s in Cleveland—the president of a new University. In theory, the Cleveland University would be perched above the Cuyahoga River Valley. While a picturesque setting, this location meant that the institution was too far removed from the city's population. The original plan was for a university where students lived among the greater community, thus cementing ties and creating mutual benefit for town and gown. In practice the bucolic site seemed a world away from the city. There was no direct roadway or bridge into Cleveland at the time. Had the endeavor been self-sustaining, it may have worked, but its unique aim to host many areas of specialization within reach of an urban population was undermined by geography.[4]

It did not help the new university that Mahan left Oberlin on such bad terms. When representatives of Cleveland University solicited funds from donors who traditionally supported Oberlin, the older school reacted. Someone from Oberlin College made public previously private documents related to the controversies of 1850. This gave supporters of the new university pause, and several withdrew financial support or pledges. In December 1852 Asa Mahan resigned from Cleveland University. The period between January 1853 and late 1855 were lean years for Mahan.

---

3   William H. Seward, *Speech of William H. Seward, on the Admission of California. Delivered in the Senate of the United States, March 11, 1850* (Washington, DC: Buell & Blanchard, 1850).

4   Madden and Hamilton, *Freedom and Grace: The Life of Asa Mahan*, 127–46.

The former president supported his family through preaching engagements, lectures, and writing.[5]

Then in October of 1855 Asa Mahan was called to be the pastor of a Congregational church in Jackson, Michigan. He served in this capacity until the spring of 1858. While not a long tenure, Mahan's years in Jackson appear to have been reasonably tranquil. He embraced the traditional role of pastor, and his parishioners seemed to appreciate his work. He never did eliminate the itch for an academic post, and before long he was involved in surrounding colleges as a guest lecturer. One institution in particular attracted his attention.[6]

Michigan Union College was a very small school located a few miles east of Jackson in Leoni. Founded in 1845 by abolitionist Wesleyan Methodists, this environment offered Mahan a new opportunity to engage pressing issues. He spent time among the student literary societies at Michigan Union as a speaker, and he almost certainly learned anew the concerns of young people. Literary societies in general were an excellent context for meeting the next generation of thinkers, and though small, Michigan Union had its own forums for debate.[7]

Mahan's nomadic pattern took another turn in the spring of 1858. He received a call to the Plymouth Congregational Church, Adrian, Michigan. For the first time in a long time, Asa Mahan was not leaving trouble behind. Rather, he was moving to a somewhat bigger town with a congregation known for openness and for supporting free speech. In retrospect, it may seem rather odd that a decade marked by intense national conflict would be a time when Mahan's personal commitments kept him, for the most part, out of public life. He had been active among some conferences and humanitarian work while in Jackson. Yet the move to Adrian soon before the Civil War amplified his vocation as an abolitionist.[8]

---

5 Madden and Hamilton, 127–46.
6 Madden and Hamilton, 147–52.
7 Madden and Hamilton, 151.
8 Madden and Hamilton, 152–55.

Asa Mahan was a serial college planter, and not long after arriving in Adrian he joined an effort to start a new college there. The endeavor was not without drama. It essentially involved moving the core of then struggling Michigan Union College from Leoni to Adrian—a distance of some forty miles. Overtures to Michigan Union ignited a bidding war between the cities of Jackson and Adrian. Would Michigan Union stay in Jackson County, with renewed support from the nearest city, or would it pick up and go a bit south and east to Adrian?

Lenawee County, Michigan, where Adrian is located, had roughly 38,000 residents at the time, a substantial number for the region and era. Moreover, Adrian was, according to some estimates, the second largest city in the state—after Detroit. During early 1859 public meetings were held in Adrian to test the waters. Could they raise enough funds to woo Michigan Union College? The short answer: "yes." By the middle of March, $30,000 had been raised. Because Michigan Union represented the antislavery Wesleyan Methodist Connection, six trustees for Adrian College would come from this body. Another six would be elected from the community of Adrian. The new institution was designed as a church/town partnership.[9]

Two buildings were soon constructed. They would serve as residence halls for men and women respectively, and twelve trustees were selected. Not surprisingly, Asa Mahan was elected as both president and as Professor of Intellectual and Moral Science. After anticipating an earlier start, officials decided to open the college on December 1, 1859. A small cadre of faculty was hired, and students were recruited. Some were to come from Michigan Union and finish their degrees in Adrian. Others would begin college at the new location. Tradition (legend, really) holds that at least some of the college equipment from Michigan Union, along with the literary society libraries, were transported by oxcart to Adrian in the

---

9   A. Douglas MacNaughton, *A History of Adrian College* (Adrian, Michigan: Adrian College, 1994), 7–9.

middle of the night. To this day the "oxcart" remains a symbol of Adrian College's determination and its commitment to literary endeavors.[10]

What Christian Duty Required Him to Do

The first months of study at Adrian revolved around the calendar year more than the traditional academic year. There was activity in late 1859, with especially powerful dialogue and debate among the new literary society, but it was not until the spring of 1860 that the school gained traction. The first available college catalogue, printed for the 1860/1861 academic year, shows that the new school was heavily dependent upon its preparatory department for enrollment. Among the four-year college course, there were three seniors, seven juniors, eleven sophomores, and twenty-four freshmen.[11]

As planned, twelve people served on the board of trustees, some with notable resumes as antislavery advocates. For instance, Fitch Reed (1814–1897) was a farmer from Cambridge Township in Lenawee County (northwest of Adrian).[12] A dedicated Wesleyan Methodist, he served as one of the region's chief hosts on the Underground Railroad. During April of 1853 Reed and his wife Ann supported a well-documented adventure in freedom. "The Escape of the Twenty-Eight" was a harrowing journey of people from Boone County, Kentucky—through Cincinnati—up the eastern border of Indiana and into Michigan, before crossing the Detroit River.

Near the end of their sojourn, the travelers were given shelter on Reed's farm. Later Reed documented the way a profane character named John Fairfield helped lead the group: "There was a reward out for him [Fairfield] of $500, dead or alive. Four teams from my house (in Cambridge, Mich.) started at sunset, drove through Clinton after dark, got to

---

10 McNaughton, 6–9.

11 *Catalogue of the Officers and Students of Adrian College, 1860–61* (Adrian, Michigan: S. P. Jermain & Co., Book and Job Printers, 1861), 9–11.

12 *Catalogue of the Officers and Students of Adrian College, 1860–61*, 5.

Ypsilanti before daylight."[13] From Ypsilanti, Michigan, the group pressed on toward Detroit and the river crossing.

Reed was representative of the people who formed Adrian College. Born in Ontario County, New York, he demonstrated the continuing influence of that region's evangelicals. Moreover, Reed was raised some sixty miles east of Asa Mahan's boyhood home. When folks settled in Lenawee County, Michigan, they brought a lot of New York State antislavery culture with them.

Mahan and Reed were by no means the only New York antislavery people to rally around Adrian College. The first annual commencement of the institution took place on Tuesday, June 12, 1860. It was a commencement in word only. No degrees were granted. Regardless, the occasion included a placing of the cornerstone for the College chapel, and celebrated Wesleyan Methodist abolitionist Luther Lee was brought to town for the keynote address.[14]

This was the same Luther Lee from New York State who argued "the supremacy of the divine law."[15] During the 1850s he spent a brief period as professor of theology at Michigan Union College in Leoni. The timing of his June 1860 Adrian College address spoke volumes. By July 4 of that year Luther Lee stood in North Elba, New York, at the grave of recently executed abolitionist John Brown.

Historians are still divided over the mental stability and purposes of John Brown. A rabid abolitionist, he participated in the murder of proslavery people in Kansas. During 1858 he began planning the takeover of the federal arsenal at Harpers Ferry, Virginia (present-day West Virginia). On October 16, 1859, Brown and a small "army" took Harpers Ferry by storm. They hoped to start an uprising of enslaved people—in effect to wage a

---

13 Fitch Reed, letter to Wilbur H. Siebert, March 23, 1893. Wilbur H. Siebert Collection, Box 48 (Columbus: Ohio Historical Society).

14 A. Douglas MacNaughton, *A History of Adrian College*, 10. See also the newspaper coverage in the *Adrian Daily Expositor*, Tuesday Evening, June 12, 1860, 1, and the *Adrian Daily Expositor*, Wednesday Evening, June 13, 1860, 1.

15 Lee, *Five Sermons and a Tract*, 43–57.

war for freedom among that mountainous region. However, their plan and assault fell to pieces when they found themselves pinned down. Finally, a contingent of United States marines under the command of Robert E. Lee attacked, killing many of the raiders and wounding Brown. John Brown was tried for treason and convicted. He was hanged on December 2, 1859. The day after Adrian College officially began offering classes, this enigmatic captain died on the gallows.[16]

Luther Lee's July 4, 1860, speech at John Brown's grave was a ringing endorsement of the violent abolitionist. He considered Brown a martyr. Lee's autobiography recalled:

> I preached and published a funeral sermon for John Brown, whom brave old Virginia, who never tires, succeeded in hanging. He was buried in North Elba, in north-eastern New York, by the side of a rock under the shadow of the Adirondack Mountains. Wendell Phillips delivered an oration over his grave when he was buried. He had a little home in this wild region on a piece of land which had been given him by Gerrit Smith. On the 4th of July, 1860, I was called from my home in Ohio to deliver an oration from the rock overhanging John Brown's grave. That was the oration of my life, the most radical and, probably, the most able I ever delivered.[17]

"Radical" might even be an understatement. On August 3, 1860, *The Liberator* published excerpts of the speech. One notable quip by Lee read something like this: "These views may be regarded as too radical and revolutionary. If they are revolutionary, they are suited to the necessities of these times, for what is wrong needs revolutionizing."[18] During the Civil War, Luther Lee joined the faculty at Adrian College.

---

16 See Michael S. Green, *Politics and America in Crisis: The Coming of the Civil War*, 144–46.

17 Luther Lee, *Autobiography of the Rev. Luther Lee, D.D.* (New York: Phillips & Hunt, 1882), 295.

18 Luther Lee, "Fourth of July Oration," *The Liberator* 30, no. 31 (August 3, 1860): 121.

The relationship between campus and national events would be mere coincidence, except that people like Luther Lee and others made them of one cloth. Perhaps most bracing is the activity of Adrian College students following Brown's raid. The literary societies from Michigan Union College were re-incorporated as the Star Literary Society at Adrian. During December 1859 this student forum kept careful records of its beginning, election of officers, and other organizational items. The very first debate was held on Friday, December 30, 1859. After opening exercises, the student group divided itself into teams of discourse. The statement for examination: "Resolved that John Brown in the planning and attempted execution of the Harpers Ferry Insurrection did what Christian duty required him to do."[19] It was a stunning formulation of the question. There was no attempt to evade the fact that an actual insurrection took place. Moreover, the language did not suggest that the behavior of Brown and his followers might some way be excused. Adrian College students were considering whether the whole affair was a matter of duty.

It is difficult to imagine that such a statement would garner much, if any, support, and the record hints that the discussion was robust. In the end, however, "the question was referred back to the House and adopted by a rising vote of eight against five."[20] *Adopted*. There was no sizable number on either side of the question, and the outcome was certainly more a symbolic gesture than any sort of institutional policy. Yet consider the same discussion at firebrand Oberlin College. During 1860 an Oberlin literary society debated the resolution: "Resolved, That Jno Brown should have the sympathy of true friends of freedom."[21] This rather tepid

---

19 Star Literary Society, Constitution and Bylaws, Minutes December 16, 1859–September 18, 1867, Archives, Shipman Library, Adrian College, December 30, 1859, 13.

20 Star Literary Society, Minutes, December 30, 1859, 14.

21 Robert Samuel Fletcher, *A History of Oberlin College: From Its Foundation through the Civil War*, Vol. 2, 772.

language passed by a vote of fourteen for and twelve against.[22] Adrian College promised to be an environment of steely abolitionist commitment.

Interspersed among debates regarding pressing social issues were more theoretical conversations, some directly related to moral philosophy. On December 14, 1860, the Star Society addressed the resolution: "That experience is the foundation of knowledge."[23] The motion to adopt was carried. On November 22, 1861, the organization considered the resolution: "That men are governed more by circumstances than by the will."[24] This statement was not affirmed by the group. Then on February 6, 1863, the Society debated the resolution: "That in all cases conscience is a correct moral guide."[25] A motion to adopt this statement was carried.

Overall, the records of the Star Literary Society offer a window on student sentiment regarding both questions of principle and action. As 1859 turned into 1860 and eventually into the Civil War era, the Star Literary Society topics tell quite a tale. For starters, while passionate about freedom and human dignity, this was not a pacifist community. That fact was no more apparent than during the Star Society debate of Friday, March 20, 1863. The organization confronted a resolution that simply stated: "That war is never justifiable."[26] There was only one member willing "to uphold the affirmative."[27] This particular discussion is made all the more intriguing because President Mahan was present—a rare thing over the course of his busy Civil War years. The college president had recently returned from Washington, DC, where he advocated for a particular military strategy with the Lincoln administration.

Adrian College was therefore firmly rooted in the just or justifiable war tradition. Others might wonder if this position went too far, but it

---

22 Fletcher, 772.

23 Star Literary Society, Minutes, December 16, 1859–September 18, 1867, December 14, 1860, 59.

24 Star Literary Society, Minutes, November 22, 1861, 95.

25 Star Literary Society, Minutes, February 6, 1863, 139.

26 Star Literary Society, Minutes, March 20, 1863, 145.

27 Star Literary Society, Minutes, March 20, 1863, 145.

was a reality at the new school. Some may have understood the need for armed resistance to southern slavery as a regrettable necessity, perhaps even some on campus. Yet the academic community at Adrian was not confused about its convictions. The Civil War would be a fight to preserve the Union, but it was also, for them (from the very beginning), a war to eliminate human bondage. This aim was not negotiable. Ending slavery was an absolute duty. There was something of the deontological ethic and its duty-based emphases swirling about the educational environment at Adrian College.

Slavery and the Constitution

On September 16, 2015, historian Sean Wilentz released an explosive op-ed in the pages of the *New York Times*. His argument: that the Constitution of the United States did not ever recognize human beings as property. Professor Wilentz's piece rebuffed a presidential campaign comment of Senator Bernie Sanders. The Vermont senator remarked that the United States was founded on racist principles. While it is unclear whether Sanders intended to offer a constitutional observation, Wilentz made the nation's covenant his focus in rebuttal. The professor responded: "The Civil War began over a simple question: Did the Constitution of the United States recognize slavery—property in humans—in national law?"[28] Within a day the blogosphere (and some published venues) were up for grabs. A storm of historians and commentators charged Wilentz with being naïve, at best—perhaps even duplicitous.

To make matters more interesting, Sean Wilentz was recognized for having close ties with the Clinton family. Therefore, the criticism of Sanders could not be extracted from the professor's known support for Hillary Clinton. The whole fracas revealed real-time political loyalties while presenting itself as reflection about the Constitution. The narrative went

---

28 Sean Wilentz, "Constitutionally, Slavery is No National Institution," *New York Times*, September 16, 2015, https://nti.ms/UUcVc. The print version of this column appeared on September 16, 2015, on Page A27 of the *New York Times*, under the title, "Lincoln and Douglass Had It Right."

roughly as follows: Senator Bernie Sanders dared to be the outsider, not only challenging the way the system worked but also the very foundation of the entire system. Secretary Hillary Clinton represented the establishment left, really a centrist force more than anything else. Her allies could be counted on to protect the system's foundations.

This caricature was and remains unfortunate. It loads the Constitution of the United States with contemporary political assumptions and baggage, and that document already bears more than its share of agendas. The critics of Professor Wilentz reminded him in no uncertain terms that the country did allow a vicious racism to infect its charters (a fact that Wilentz never disputed). Yet there was something to the argument that the Constitution never explicitly sanctioned property in people. The debate was heated and significant, but it was not at all new. The same intense conversation dominated the early and middle nineteenth century.

There were, to focus on the major points, at least five parts of the United States Constitution prior to 1865 that appeared to sanction slavery. Article I, Section 2, Paragraph 3 includes the infamous "three-fifths" language for certain aspects of state representation. The damning theoretical shorthand would imply that enslaved persons were considered three-fifths human. Article I, Section 9, Paragraph 1 appears to suggest that the so-called "slave trade" could not be abolished before 1808. Article I, Section 9, Paragraph 4 refers back to the "three-fifths" formula for purposes of taxation. Article IV, Section 2, Paragraph 3 would suggest that fugitives from slavery cannot receive freedom in a different state. Article V revisits both the importation of people before 1808 and the formula for taxation.

It is difficult and perhaps even disingenuous to deny that these references in the Constitution refer to slavery, at least as a kind of forced servitude. Southern powerbrokers were counting on this interpretation from the beginning. John C. Calhoun has gone down in history as the patron of proslavery constitutionalism. The more recent dissection of Calhoun's writings, especially the way he asserted that slavery was a "positive good," has garnered much attention. Yet, deep within Calhoun lived a resolute conviction that the Constitution offered federal protection for slavery. On this point he was not alone.

During February of 1847 an aging John C. Calhoun rose among the Senate to defend slavery as an institution entirely consistent with the United States Constitution. Yet he did so without citing chapter and verse of the nation's covenant. Instead he considered the instrument as a whole and argued that it was not an agreement between people so much as a compact between states:

> Ours is a Federal Constitution. The States are its constituents, and not the people. The twenty-eight States—the twenty-nine States (including Iowa)—stand, under this Government, as twenty-nine individuals, or as twenty-nine millions of individuals would stand to a consolidated power! No, Sir. It was made for higher ends. It was so formed that every State, as a constituent member of this Union of ours, should enjoy all its advantages, natural and acquired, with greater security, and enjoy them more perfectly.[29]

Calhoun was not to be outdone when it came to language of "higher" purpose and meaning, and the whole theory grounding his remarks can be attributed to "states' rights" thinking. Still, another dynamic lurked behind his words.

Calhoun was not simply claiming state prerogative against federal power. He was also dismissing the claims of individuals against state power. Later in his speech he echoed this theme: "Sir, the right of framing self-government on the part of individuals is not near so easily to be established by any course of reasoning, as the right of a community or State to self-government."[30] This ideological presumption against persons was perhaps as strong as the devotion to state supremacy. Calhoun's curious disregard for people is often missed by typical analysis that pits federal and state authority against one another.

---

29 John C. Calhoun, *The Works of John C. Calhoun*, ed. Richard K. Cralle, Vol. 4 (New York: D. Appleton and Company, 1883), 344.

30 Calhoun, *The Works of John C. Calhoun*, 345–46.

In a strange way, Calhoun's position was akin to that of abolitionist William Lloyd Garrison (1805–1879). The Boston zealot may be considered the antithesis of everything Calhoun represented, but he, like the South Carolina senator, held that the Constitution was a proslavery instrument. Garrison made this argument quite early in his career. The December 29, 1832, issue of *The Liberator* denounced the nation's covenant:

> There is much declamation about the sacredness of the compact which was formed between the free and slave states, on the adoption of the Constitution. A sacred compact, forsooth! We pronounce it the most bloody and heaven-daring arrangement ever made by men for the continuance and protection of a system of the most atrocious villany [*sic*] ever exhibited on earth. Yes—we recognize the compact, but with feelings of shame and indignation, and it will be held in everlasting infamy by the friends of justice and humanity throughout the world.[31]

Garrison became notorious for burning copies of the Constitution. His policies of non-resistance, moral suasion, and abstention from political action gave him the ambience of purity, but it was purity that came with a high price. He was willing to let the South go its way before he would fight for a free Union.

One can look at William Lloyd Garrison through a number of lenses. He might be seen as a crank, rigid and right, and this characterization was familiar to people like Asa Mahan. Yet Garrison and Mahan had completely different notions of nationhood. It is tempting to conclude that Garrison, though radical and pure, failed to appreciate the more practical aspects of abolition. This reading then portrays him as someone so rarefied that he lacked the skills necessary for making a better republic. A corollary to this view considers politically active abolitionists as more moderate, flexible, and realistic about ending slavery. To an extent, it is a time-honored and legitimate interpretation.

---

31 William Lloyd Garrison, "The Great Crisis!" *The Liberator* 2, no. 52 (December 29, 1832): 207.

However, this template does not face one important possibility. What if Garrison's theoretical principles were less laudable than supposed? In other words, perhaps Garrison was not simply a saint devoid of utility. His underlying theoretical approach may have been less than perfect. Correspondingly, those who chose to enter the political arena and fight for an entirely free Union were not necessarily compromisers. Some were as unyielding as William Lloyd Garrison. They were also unwilling to separate from the South as a way to defend the right.

None of these historical considerations settle the debate that erupted during the 2016 presidential campaign. The majority view tends to conclude that the Constitution was indeed a document that at least gave cover for slavery, even if it did not explicitly endorse the practice.[32] Yet the op-ed by Professor Wilentz, full of bombast and its own questionable assertions, contains a haunting conceptual question. Did the Constitution of the United States, as originally drafted and adopted, affirm the idea of property in human beings?

This more technical framing of the issue might be dismissed as terminological evasion or wishful thinking, a grasping at straws to claim that the Constitution was somehow antislavery. Yet , the fact that the Southern legal community built an elaborate system around the notion that enslaved people were property makes the question relevant. Through all of the euphemistic language and reference to people "held to service," did the Constitution assert that some should be considered property, things, objects owned by others? It is a fair question and one that motivated certain antebellum abolitionists. They maintained that the answer was no—the idea of property in human beings could not be found among the Constitution. These antislavery warriors were not the majority, but they meant business.

---

32 See especially the study by David Waldstreicher, *Slavery's Constitution: From Revolution to Ratification* (New York: Hill and Wang, 2009).

Antislavery Constitutionalism

It was not like Frederick Douglass to be far from the action. Yet that is where he found himself in late 1859 and early 1860. Soon after John Brown's insurrection, Douglass slipped over to Canada and on November 12, 1859, boarded a steamer for England. He was on a mission to spread the antislavery message, and this was not his first trip to the United Kingdom. He had been there in the middle 1840s, but the circumstances of this second trip were different. His name had been discovered in documents related to Brown, and authorities in Virginia were after Douglass. The complicated story of Frederick Douglass's relationship with John Brown is full of intrigue. They knew each other quite well, and Brown hoped Douglass would join his uprising. Douglass declined but supported Brown in spirit and did not share his awareness of the plot. The heat was on, and Frederick Douglass headed for England.[33]

Some four months after his arrival abroad, Douglass gave a monumental speech: "The Constitution of the United States: Is it Pro-Slavery or Antislavery?" This address was delivered in the Queen's Rooms of Glasgow's West End. The speech became a classic statement of the movement known as "antislavery constitutionalism." With signature eloquence, Frederick Douglass held forth that the Constitution of the United States was not proslavery. Rather, he claimed, it was unquestionably a charter of freedom. The address was no repetition of long-held beliefs. It was perhaps the most complete articulation of Douglass's dramatic change in thinking. He once shared the views of William Lloyd Garrison that the Constitution was riddled with proslavery sentiment, but by 1860 he stood firmly on the opposite side of the question. Why the transformation, and how did it come?

When Frederick Douglass first freed himself from slavery he found a home among New England abolitionists. In 1841 he joined Garrison's

---

33 Robert S. Levine, *The Lives of Frederick Douglass* (Cambridge: Harvard University Press, 2016), 187–95. See also James A. Colaiaco, *Frederick Douglass and the Fourth of July* (New York: Palgrave MacMillan, 2006), 164.

Massachusetts Anti-Slavery Society, and soon he became a popular orator on the speaking circuit. It meant something to be a person with firsthand experience of human bondage. Douglass possessed immediate credibility. The predominantly white audiences were hungry for his accounts of suffering and cruelty in the South.[34]

Garrison and others who shared the philosophy of moral suasion and abstention from political involvement were captivated by Frederick Douglass. He, in turn, was drawn to their organization and commitment. Yet over the 1840s, Douglass developed a systematic critique of slavery. He did not wish to be an exhibit of cruelty. He knew himself as the intellectual equal of any person. His second autobiography, *My Bondage and My Freedom* (1855), explained:

> Among the first duties assigned me, on entering the ranks, was to travel, in company with Mr. George Foster, to secure subscribers to the "Anti-slavery Standard" and the "Liberator." With him I traveled and lectured through the eastern counties of Massachusetts. Much interest was awakened—large meetings assembled. Many came, no doubt, from curiosity to hear what a negro could say in his own cause. I was generally introduced as a "*chattel*"—a "*thing*"—a piece of southern "*property*"—the chairman assuring the audience that *it* could speak.[35]

White New England abolitionists wished to mock the Southern legal philosophy of property in people. They oftentimes could not or would not confront their own objectifying behavior. When Douglass elaborated upon his experience by analyzing and denouncing slavery he was taken to task by his "friends." They would make the philosophical arguments. Frederick Douglass was there to narrate a story of victimization.[36]

---

34 Colaiaco, *Frederick Douglass and the Fourth of July*, 12–17.
35 Douglass, *My Bondage and My Freedom in Frederick Douglass Autobiographies*, 366.
36 Douglass, 367.

Whether addressing obvious forms of racism or its more subtle, self-righteous expressions, issues of basic personhood drove Douglass's witness. Later, in 1854, he offered a methodically reasoned argument, "The Claims of the Negro, Ethnologically Considered," and he felt compelled to begin with a sad observation: "The first general claim which may here be set up, respects the manhood of the negro. This is an elementary claim, simple enough, but not without question. It is fiercely opposed."[37] It was also a claim that shaped his attitude toward the United States Constitution.

For a while Douglass kept an uneasy peace with Garrison's movement, and he even repeated the typical New England criticisms of the United States Constitution. During August 1847 Garrison and Douglass traveled together to the Oberlin Collegiate Institute. They debated Asa Mahan and others regarding whether Christian abolitionists should "come out" of the established church, and they debated the Constitution. Garrison recalled the engagement (held in the presence of almost three thousand people) in a letter to his wife:

> Douglass and myself have done nearly all the talking, on our side, friend Foster [Stephen Foster] saying but little. The principal topics of discussion have been Come-outerism from the Church and the State. Pres. Mahan entered into the debate in favor of the U. S. Constitution as an anti-slavery instrument, and, consequently, of the Liberty Party. He was perfectly respectful, and submitted to our interrogations with good temper and courtesy. As a disputant, he is adroit and plausible, but neither vigorous nor profound.[38]

The relationship between Mahan and Garrison was strained, at best.

Not long after visiting Oberlin, Frederick Douglass moved to Rochester, New York, and began his own publication, *The North Star.* This

---

37 Frederick Douglass, "The Claims of the Negro, Ethnologically Considered. An Address, Before the Literary Societies of Western Reserve College, at Commencement, July 12, 1854" (Rochester: Lee, Mann & Co., 1854), 6.

38 Wendell P. Garrison, *William Lloyd Garrison, 1805–1879: The Story of His Life,* Vol. 3 (New York: The Century Co., 1889), 203.

striking out to the west promised freedom and independence that Douglass had not enjoyed in Massachusetts. He was joined in the publishing business by Pittsburgh physician and newspaper editor Martin Delany (1812–1885). The formal association between the two was short-lived, but Delany wove himself in and out of many abolitionist circles over the next several decades.[39]

Douglass's views regarding the Constitution did not change immediately. Yet over time and after critical study he came to conclude that the United States Constitution was essentially an antislavery instrument. The decade of the 1850s allowed him to hone this perspective, and by 1860 his considered argument was ready for major presentation.

To a great extent, western New York was the cradle of antislavery constitutionalism. Here and in the state's central parts were voices that had long been politically active and theoretically committed to an antislavery reading of the nation's covenant. Lysander Spooner (1808–1887) was perhaps the most systematic mind making the case for an antislavery Constitution, and he was unusual in more than one respect. Spooner hailed from New England, but his legal theories motivated the politically dedicated abolitionists of New York. In 1845 he wrote a tightly reasoned treatise, *The Unconstitutionality of Slavery*. Others of this school were more closely attached to New York State. William Goodell (1792–1878) was a Liberty Party leader who wrote *Views of American Constitutional Law, in Its Bearing upon American Slavery* (1844). Yet Gerrit Smith (1797–1874) of Peterboro, New York, probably topped them all.

Smith was another Liberty Party legend with ties to Oberlin—as well as John Brown. Like Douglass, Smith was implicated in the Harpers Ferry insurrection. He was also very wealthy and had a record of funding many abolitionist causes, including Frederick Douglass's *North Star*. Perhaps the most profound influence that Smith brought to Douglass was an

---

39 Louis Rosenfeld, "Martin Robison Delany (1812–1885): Physician, Black Separatist, Explorer, Soldier," *Bulletin of the New York Academy of Medicine* 65, no. 7 (September 1989): 802.

antislavery reading of the Constitution.[40] Finally, on May 15, 1851, Douglass made a clean break with Garrison and endorsed antislavery constitutionalism. He wrote in *The North Star*: "The change in our opinion on this subject has not been hastily arrived at. A careful study of the writings of Lysander Spooner, of Gerrit Smith, and of William Goodell, has brought us to our present conclusion."[41] Douglass was well-informed, but the independent findings were his own. William Lloyd Garrison was not delighted.

By March 26, 1860, when Frederick Douglass addressed his audience at Glasgow's Queen's Rooms, his conviction had been forged in many fires. Douglass articulated an interpretive approach that was sacred to antislavery constitutionalists. The particulars of the document were to be read through the prism of its preamble. Beyond that, the Constitution was to be understood on its own terms. Arguments about its meaning should not revolve around background narratives or notes from the Constitutional Convention. It was the final product, as ratified, that counted: "Again, it should be borne in mind that the mere text, and only the text, and not any commentaries or creeds written by those who wished to give the text a meaning apart from its plain reading, was adopted as the Constitution of the United States."[42] If there was to be any presumption, it should lean toward protection of natural rights.

---

40 Colaiaco, *Frederick Douglass and the Fourth of July*, 82. See also the fascinating popular treatment of Gerrit Smith's connection to John Brown: Jan Bridgeford-Smith, "Money, Morality, and Madness: Businessman Gerrit Smith Gambled it All on John Brown," *America's Civil War*, September 2015, 48–53.

41 Frederick Douglass, *The North Star*, May 15, 1851. Extract reprinted in *The Liberator* 21, no. 21 (May 23, 1851): 82.

42 Frederick Douglass, *Selected Speeches and Writings*, Philip S. Foner, ed., Abridged and Adapted by Yuval Taylor (Chicago: Lawrence Hill Books, 1999), 381. Any exploration of common threads among antislavery constitutionalists must begin with William M. Wiecek's groundbreaking study: *The Sources of Antislavery Constitutionalism in America, 1760–1848* (Ithaca: Cornell University Press, 1977).

Douglass made much of the difference between persons and things. He employed the distinction to argue against the belief that there existed any notion of property in people throughout the Constitution: "If there are two ideas more distinct in their character and essence than another, those ideas are 'persons' and 'property,' 'men' and 'things.' Now, when it is proposed to transform persons into 'property' and men into beasts of burden, I demand that the law that contemplates such a purpose shall be expressed with irresistible clearness."[43] The language of "irresistible clearness" was used by many antislavery constitutionalists and reflected a Supreme Court case from 1805. This terminology had been wielded with great effect by Lysander Spooner in his book, *The Unconstitutionality of Slavery.*[44]

Combining the interpretive priority of the Constitution's preamble and the concern for personhood Douglass thundered:

Its language is "we the people"; not we the white people, not even we the citizens, not we the privileged class, not we the high, not we the low, but we the people; not we the horses, sheep, and swine, and wheel-barrows, but we the people, we the human inhabitants; and, if Negroes are people, they are included in the benefits for which the Constitution of America was ordained and established.[45]

This sentence became the most memorable and probably most quoted statement of the address. Frederick Douglass spoke for many who would not give up on either the Constitution or each and every person under its care.

Seven Golden Candlesticks

On Friday evening, September 19, 1862, the students of Adrian College's Star Literary Society filed into their room for weekly exercises. The meeting was called to order by Philip Dowling. Henry Wright offered a

---

43 Douglass, 387.

44 Lysander Spooner, *The Unconstitutionality of Slavery* (Boston: Bela Marsh, 1845), 22.

45 Douglass, *Selected Speeches and Writings*, 387.

prayer. Emma Spencer and one of the Bertram sisters read selections, and E. S. Todd delivered an oration on "Michigan and Her History." Mary Backus (soon to be the first woman graduate of Adrian College) gave a recitation. Then the gathering got down to business. It was time for debate. The query: "Is the Constitution of the United States an antislavery document?" We do not know the details of the argument, but we do know that after a lengthy contest "the question was decided in the affirmative."[46] Adrian College students were on the side of antislavery constitutionalism.

The student verdict was not necessarily surprising, but as a matter of context it should be noted that this discussion took place between two extraordinary events. On Wednesday, September 17, George B. McClellan's army clashed with that of Robert E. Lee along Maryland's Antietam Creek. Federal casualties numbered 12,469. Confederate casualties were estimated at 13,724.[47] Often considered the bloodiest single day of the Civil War, this less-than-decisive engagement was used by Abraham Lincoln to make a bold claim. On Monday, September 22, the nation's chief executive issued his Preliminary Emancipation Proclamation. Two days following the Battle of Antietam and roughly two days before the president's bombshell announcement, a group of Adrian College students declared that the Constitution of the United States was an antislavery instrument.

Several young men had left Adrian in 1861 to fight for the Union. The Fourth Michigan Infantry was organized and trained on campus, not a stone's throw from the chapel. Many who knew the tight-knit environs of Adrian's Madison Street were now in the Maryland Campaign, and those left behind did not arrive at their views regarding the Constitution in a vacuum.

---

46 Star Literary Society, Minutes, September 19, 1862, 118.

47 E. B. Long with Barbara Long, *The Civil War Day by Day: An Almanac, 1861–1865*, foreword by Bruce Catton (Garden City, New York: Doubleday & Company, Inc., 1971), 267–68.

The first Adrian College catalogue lists a course on "Constitutional and International Law," offered during the second term of the senior year.[48] A major portion of Asa Mahan's personal notebook of lecture outlines contains detailed commentary on the Constitution, and evidence reveals that he espoused these views by the middle and late 1840s. One year before William Lloyd Garrison and Frederick Douglass debated Mahan at Oberlin (1847), two others had come for a similar exchange of views. Stephen and Abby Kelley Foster (associates of Garrison) were in Oberlin during the autumn of 1846, and one of their main questions for debate with Mahan asked: "Is the Constitution of the United States a pro-slavery document?"[49] The proceedings received a comprehensive review in *The Oberlin Evangelist*.

The paper's recapitulation of the debate reads like a page out of Lysander Spooner. Asa Mahan argued that, since there was no explicit mention of slavery in the Constitution, it should be construed as a document that did not recognize bondage. *The Evangelist* summarized his major thrust:

> Hence, the legal interpreter must always lean towards the side of human rights—towards liberty, and against Slavery. It is horrible to presume an intention to rob and enslave;—hence nothing but imperative necessity can justify you in admitting such a presumption. Hence of two possible constructions of a legal document, whether a constitution or a statute, that which is favorable to human rights must always be adopted—that which is adverse must be rejected. Nothing less than "irresistible clearness" can be held sufficient to warrant a construction which involves the intention of infringing rights and trampling down justice.[50]

Once again, the United States Supreme Court decision of 1805 (United States versus Fisher) was invoked. Additionally, Mahan followed

---

48 *Catalogue of the Officers and Students of Adrian College, 1860–61* (Adrian, Michigan: S. P. Jermain & Co., Book and Job Printers, 1861), 20, 22.

49 "American Slavery a System of Illegal Usurpation," *The Oberlin Evangelist* 8, no. 20 (September 30, 1846): 158.

50 "American Slavery a System of Illegal Usurpation," 158.

Spooner's contention that slavery never really held legal standing within the United States—not during the time of colonial rule nor during later eras of the Republic. The presence of slavery did not mean it was protected by law. Slavery's existence was, at best, a *de facto* reality—not a *de jure* reality.[51]

Mahan's argument in this 1846 debate came only two years following the publication of William Goodell's book on constitutional interpretation and a mere one year following the release of Spooner's text. He wasted no time in doing his homework. Through the 1850s and up to the Civil War, Mahan polished his stance. Several pages before his detailed commentary on the Constitution, Mahan's personal notebook contains a curt, fifteen-point outline in favor of antislavery constitutionalism. The very first claim states: "The idea of property in man not in the constitution."[52] This fundamental conviction is followed by several standard arguments. For instance, Mahan stressed that only reference to secondary notes or memories of the Constitutional Convention could establish any connection between slavery and the document. Moreover, positive law recognizing slavery must be expressed with "irresistible clearness," and since such explicit language was missing, the instrument could not be interpreted as protecting bondage.[53]

However, Asa Mahan's most complete and unique commentary on the Constitution occupies the closing portion of his notebook—specifically pages 218–81. Here he made the preamble of the text his hermeneutical key. This was a routine strategy among antislavery constitutionalists, but Mahan employed the method in philosophically significant ways. He defined a preamble as "the motives, aims, & object of the whole instrument."[54] From the standpoint of philosophy, the preamble was all about ends desired. He continued: "Of two interpretations, one compatible & the

---

51 "American Slavery a System of Illegal Usurpation," 158.
52 Asa Mahan, "Manuscript Writings, Miscellaneous," Archives, Shipman Library, Adrian College, Page 199.
53 Mahan, 199–200.
54 Mahan, 222.

other incompatible with the spirit & aim of the whole instrument, as set forth in the preamble, the former is to be adopted."[55] This subjected every part of the Constitution to the ends outlined within its preamble.

Just what were these identified ends? Mahan began by rebuking the ideology of John C. Calhoun and others:

> It is not as states, but as a people, that this Constitution was ordained & established. The instrument goes back of & beneath all existing State or Colonial organizations, to the formation & source of all governmental authority, the people, & lays the foundation of the government there.[56]

He soon followed: "Our government is, in no sense or form, a compact among states to be dissolved at the will of any of the contracting parties."[57] So much for so-called "states' rights."

When itemizing the aims or ends of the preamble, Mahan offered a brief interpretation of the six objects listed: union, justice, domestic tranquility, common defense, general welfare, and the blessings of liberty. Yet, a curious dynamic appears among his notes when listing the preamble's components. He numbered them, beginning with "We, the people of the United States."[58] Then he listed the subsequent six aims. This meant that at the end of his opening remarks he had seven, not six, critical categories. In other words, he included the living agents, the actors or subjects of the nation, along with the six aims or objects. To summarize his remarks, Mahan concluded: "We find ourselves standing in the midst of seven golden candlesticks each shedding a divine light upon what government should be & enabling us to determine the intrinsic nature & character of the instrument itself, & its adaptations as a whole, to ensure its own

---

55 Mahan, 222.
56 Mahan, 222.
57 Mahan, 222.
58 Mahan, 222.

high ends."[59] The language regarding candlesticks is derived from Revelation 1:12-13.

One can almost climb inside Mahan's head here. He seems to have surprised himself by ending up with seven and not six crucial items. He did so, of course, because he began not with the desired ends but with the people—all of the people—who were to participate in creating the ends. It is no stretch to read this as a Kantian instinct. At the very least, it is counter to the kind of consequentialism that would name six ends and not be concerned with the value of the agents creating or affected by those ends. "We, the people" were not merely a means to someone else's end.

To See the Heavens Opened

During the fall of 1861, Martin Delany (former editorial partner of Frederick Douglass) returned from a trip to Africa. The Civil War had been raging for six months when Delany proposed a bold plan. According to his biographer: "As early as October, 1861, Dr. Delany, when *en route* to Chicago, stopped at Adrian, Michigan, for the purpose of seeing President Mahan, of the Michigan College. The subject of the war, which was then being earnestly waged, instantly became the theme of conversation, and the role of the colored American as an actor on its board was the principal feature therein. How and what to do to obtain admission to the service, was the question to which Dr. Delany demanded a solution."[60] Delany had a specific proposal. He aimed to raise a military unit modeled after the Zouaves d'Afrique. In the American conflict such a force would be known as a corps

---

59 Mahan, 227.

60 Frank A. Rollin, *Life and Public Services of Martin R. Delany* (Boston: Lee and Shepard, 1883; New York: Arno Press and The New York Times, 1969), 141. The first edition was published in 1883, and Frank A. Rollin was in fact Frances Ann Rollin, a woman of color who left a brilliant legacy of literary achievement and political advocacy in Reconstruction South Carolina. See Willard B. Gatewood Jr., "'The Remarkable Misses Rollin': Black Women in Reconstruction South Carolina," *The South Carolina Historical Magazine* 92, no. 3 (July 1991): 172–88.

d'Afrique. Asa Mahan liked the idea and pledged support. Unfortunately, this particular effort did not pan out, and Delany had to wait some years before entering the service. Yet it should be noted that the Delany/Mahan proposal came well before other (now-lauded) plans for African American leadership in uniform.[61]

When Martin Delany visited Adrian College, students were progressing through the year's first term. Of note were a sister and brother studying in the Junior Preparatory Department. Elizabeth and William Henry Butler called Colchester, Canada West (Ontario), home.[62] Elizabeth does not appear to have continued her course of study, but by 1864 William established himself as a campus leader. He excelled in the sciences and served as the recording secretary for the Star Literary Society.

The Butlers were children of a father who escaped slavery in Virginia and a mother who had been an indentured person from England. After studying in Adrian, William changed his last name to Fitzbutler and preferred Henry as his first name. He attended the Detroit Medical College and then graduated from the University of Michigan Medical School. In July of 1872 Dr. Fitzbutler and his wife, Sarah McCurdy Fitzbutler, moved to Louisville, Kentucky—where she received her own medical degree. Together they established a nationally recognized practice.[63]

Though a very small place, Adrian College served as an impressive incubator for equal opportunity. Students, as well as the college president, were eager to make the rest of society reflect these values, and the whole Mahan family embraced this mission. Mary and Asa Mahan's son Theodore enlisted in the Sixteenth Michigan Volunteer Infantry as an officer.

Soon after the September 1862 Battle of Antietam, young Mahan found himself heading for Fredericksburg, Virginia. The Sixteenth Michigan

---

61 Rollin, *Life and Public Services of Martin R. Delany*, 141–44.

62 *Third Annual Catalogue of Adrian College. Officers and Students for the Academical Year 1861–2* (Chicago: Church, Goodman & Cushing, Book and Job Printers, 1861), 15–16.

63 Leslie L. Hanawalt, "Henry Fitzbutler: Detroit's First Black Medical Student," *Detroit in Perspective: A Journal of Regional History* 1 (Winter, 1973): 126–40.

Meeting room of the Adrian College Star Literary Society.
Courtesy of Adrian College Shipman Library.

was in the Army of the Potomac, recently entrusted to the command of General Ambrose Burnside. In November, the Union forces gathered on high ground, across the Rappahannock River from Fredericksburg. Had they possessed the necessary pontoons, they could have crossed the river, entered the town, and pushed past any opposition on their way toward Richmond. However, battles seldom unfold as imagined. The requisite bridges did not arrive until almost December. By then Robert E. Lee's Confederate army was dug in along the heights beyond Fredericksburg. The Union forces would have to slug their way through town and through impregnable defenses on the far side of the city.[64]

---

64 Asa Mahan, *A Critical History of the Late American War* (New York: A. S. Barnes & Co., 1877), 209–15. See also the regimental summary in Jno. Robertson, *Michigan in the War*, rev. ed. (Lansing: W. S. George & Co., State Printers and Binders, 1882), 359–73.

Dr. Henry Fitzbutler, nationally acclaimed African American physician from Adrian College. Portrait by artist Naida Willette Page. Originally featured on the cover of the Journal of the National Medical Association, September 1952. Courtesy of the Journal of the National Medical Association.

An ominous fog covered the ground around Fredericksburg on the morning of December 13, 1862. General Burnside sent wave after wave of his army across the river, into the city, and up the open slope leading to Marye's Heights, where a determined and gritty foe waited. It was murder from the beginning. There was no taking the heights. Late in the day, after officers and men recognized the futility of assault, the Sixteenth Michigan, along with others in their division, attacked. Theodore Mahan was gravely wounded. According to his father: "Our only son held his company in one of those lines until he was hit by a rifle bullet, and was then thrown ten feet into the air by a large clod of earth hurled against his breast by a cannon ball which struck the ground near him. For some time

Theodore Mahan, son of Mary and Asa Mahan, killed during the Civil War. Courtesy of the Archives of Michigan's Collections.

he lay upon the spot where he fell, apparently dead."[65] Eventually, young Theodore was evacuated.

Asa Mahan had always fancied himself a military strategist. According to his telling, he opened communication with the Lincoln administration soon after the disastrous defeat of the Union army at the First Battle of Bull Run (Manassas), July 1861.[66] Mahan's strong personality no doubt made him a rather taxing correspondent, but some in Washington were willing to listen. Very late in October of 1862 Salmon P. Chase (Secretary of the Treasury) was reported to have replied: "I shall be glad to receive any practical suggestions you may make. They will be instructive to me, and may be useful to the country."[67] Fredericksburg was the last straw, and Mahan

---

65 Mahan, *A Critical History of the Late American War*, 214.

66 Mahan, 231.

67 Quoted in Mahan, *A Critical History of the Late American War*, 232.

"determined to visit Washington."[68] He would present a war strategy to the President of the United States and to the Secretary of War.

Asa Mahan left Adrian very late in December 1862 and soon arrived in the nation's capital. He actually met with several senators, as well as Abraham Lincoln. There is evidence that, after some days of meetings, Lincoln accepted Mahan's military plan, but Secretary of War Edwin Stanton and General Henry Halleck shelved the proposal. In essence, Mahan sketched a strategy for defeating the primary Confederate armies, as opposed to aiming for the capture of major cities.[69] It all sounds rather far-fetched, except that others were witness to this lobbying effort. As late as 1928 the son of Mahan's good friend, Rev. John Scott, remembered the college president staying overnight at his boyhood home in Pittsburgh while heading to Washington. Mahan stayed again a few weeks later, on return to Adrian. Young Scott recalled seeing the document that Mahan had presented to Lincoln—complete with Abraham Lincoln's signed endorsement.[70]

Following his grievous wounds, Captain Theodore Mahan was taken to the home of his sister, Anna Mahan North, in Cleveland. It was hoped that a long convalescence might enable recovery. His mother and father spent much time with him throughout the winter and spring, but he died on June 23, 1863. Mary Dix Mahan died in the fall of 1863. To compound this symphony of grief, a daughter of Mary and Asa Mahan—Elizabeth— then died. One can only imagine the unrelenting trauma such loss brings.[71]

Sometime during these excruciating Civil War years, Asa Mahan began lecturing on the Holy Spirit. His book, *The Baptism of the Holy Ghost* (1870), gathered the substance of these talks, reflecting student

---

68 Mahan, 232.

69 Mahan, 231–43.

70 W. A. S., "Stanton Said 'No': Lincoln's Indorsement Did Not Impress His Secretary of War, Dr. Mahan Found," *New York Tribune*, February 8, 1928.

71 Madden and Hamilton, *Freedom and Grace: The Life of Asa Mahan*, 171–75. *Seventy-Fifth Anniversary General Catalogue of Oberlin College, 1833–1908*, 636.

instruction from the early 1860s.[72] We will probably never know the connection between Mahan's wartime heartbreak and this text. Discourse X bears the title: "The Consolation of the Spirit, or the Uses of Afflictive Providences." The biblical grounding for this consideration of suffering is taken from Isaiah 48: "I have chosen thee in the furnace of affliction" (KJV). Yet even here, among a work devoted to the power of the Holy Spirit, Mahan revealed his moral and philosophical convictions.

Discourse IX, "The Fellowship of the Spirit," contains a fascinating definition of authentic fellowship. Mahan chose three terms to differentiate between lower and higher forms of relationship. The first was "companionship," which he considered little more than being in the same place at the same time. The second and higher expression was "partnership." This he described as "co-operation for the promotion of common ends."[73] Today many might consider this the zenith of any relationship, but Asa Mahan believed there was something both higher and deeper. This he termed "fellowship," and he described it as an empathy and reverence where "each becomes to the other, as it were, another self."[74] The distinction between partnership and fellowship is, in essence, a distinction between relationships that are conditioned by a search for some common end and relationships that are unconditional. In short, partnership had a consequentialist component. Fellowship represented a universal treatment of others as ends in themselves. The Categorical Imperative was hovering in the background of Asa Mahan's approach to the Holy Spirit. Put in more communal terms, Mahan's theology of relationships embraced something akin to Immanuel Kant's "realm of ends." Admittedly, this was an exceedingly high standard for social and political life.

---

72 Asa Mahan to Phoebe Palmer, May 4, 1870, "Palmer Family Papers, Drew University Library, Madison, New Jersey." Some years after publication, *The Baptism of the Holy Ghost* served as a critical primer for the development of Pentecostal theology. See Donald W. Dayton, *Theological Roots of Pentecostalism* (Metuchen, New Jersey: The Scarecrow Press, 1987).

73 Mahan, *The Baptism of the Holy Ghost*, 152.

74 Mahan, 153.

When Theodore Mahan died, his father described the departure in these terms: "He seemed to 'see the heavens opened, and the Son of Man standing on the right hand of God,' the Son of Man holding out to the dying one 'a crown of life.' "[75] This reference is to the epiphany given Stephen at his time of martyrdom (Acts 7:56). Those who pursue justice work from a glimpse of God's inevitable triumph. Once again, we are reminded that experience may tell us what *is* but not necessarily what *ought* to be—or what *will* be. The seers among us strain to live God's future in the now, and they often pay a tremendous price for their vision.

---

75 Mahan, *Out of Darkness into Light; or, The Hidden Life Made Manifest*, 302.

EPILOGUE

And the Days of Thy Mourning Shall be Ended

Technically speaking, the 281-page personal notebook of Asa Mahan is 280 pages long, with the final notes scribbled on the inside back cover (hence 281 pages of writing). This is significant, because those concluding observations are in response to breathtaking developments. With no more room for writing, the college president observed the passage of the Constitution's Thirteenth Amendment. For the record, that simple but monumental text reads:

> *Section 1.* Neither slavery nor involuntary servitude, except as punishment for crime whereof the party shall have been duly convicted, shall exist within the United States, or any place subject to their jurisdiction.
>
> *Section 2.* Congress shall have power to enforce this article by appropriate legislation.

The amendment passed Congress in early 1865 and was ratified December 18, 1866.

On the inside back cover of his notebook, Mahan put it this way:

Last Amendment
1.   Prohibits slavery in all its forms.

2. Imparts to congress the specific power to pass all laws requisite to secure individuals in their rights to life, liberty, & the pursuit of happiness.[1]

Unlike the actual amendment, Mahan reminds us—through language from the Declaration of Independence—that the elimination of slavery is essential to life, liberty, and the pursuit of happiness. We recall his language regarding the whole purpose of the Constitution: "Government, to answer its ends, must be the citadel of liberty to all its subjects & render each & all free & equal in the enjoyment of life, liberty & in the pursuit of happiness."[2] Asa Mahan thought the Constitution of the United States stood for these principles without a Thirteenth Amendment, but he celebrated the more explicit language when it was added to the instrument.

The almost dramatic scribbling on the inside back cover of this notebook raises a huge question. Did Asa Mahan consider the matter settled? It would appear that he did, but subsequent years have reminded us of the staying power possessed by injustice. Perhaps, once more, Mahan got ahead of himself when he declared an end to the issue—which leaves us with a haunting legacy and a very uncomfortable calling. We can hardly blame the Old Doctor for feeling vindicated and for reaching toward the ultimate resolution—even seeing it on the horizon if not fully realized during his time. However, the fact remains that the same tensions that gave rise to his life of advocacy are present today.

Following the Civil War, Asa Mahan served for seven years as president of Adrian College. He married again in 1866; and in the mid-1870s, the Mahans traveled to England and became participants among the Holiness Movement there. The Old Doctor was a principal contributor to the Oxford Convention of 1874 and the Brighton Convention of 1875. He was beloved abroad for his teaching regarding "the higher life." Though advanced in age, he seemed to enjoy a whole new chapter of ministry.

---

1 Asa Mahan, "Manuscript Writings, Miscellaneous" Archives, Shipman Library, Adrian College, Page 281.

2 Mahan, 227.

The Mahans moved to Eastbourne, England, in 1884 and continued a limited leadership among the region's revivals. On April 4, 1889, Asa Mahan went to glory, surrounded by his wife and friends. He was buried in Ocklynge Cemetery, and friends donated money for his gravestone. Among the inscription were words drawn from Isaiah 60:20: "Thy sun shall no more go down; neither shall thy moon withdraw itself: for the LORD shall be thine everlasting light, and the days of thy mourning shall be ended."[3]

A Diffuse Legacy

The legacy of Asa Mahan lives on in several places, but it is no monolithic tradition. Most think immediately of Oberlin and its social justice emphases. The Graduate School of Theology at Oberlin carried the banner forward until 1966, when it merged with the Vanderbilt Divinity School. Today signs of early Oberlin are reflected in lectureships and scholarships at Vanderbilt.[4] Oberlin College itself embraced the coming of liberal Protestantism by the early twentieth century, and today one is hard pressed to find vestiges of Asa Mahan's evangelicalism at the Ohio school.

Adrian College has taken a path that reflects the culture of many United Methodist-related institutions. Contrary to some assumptions, Adrian was not founded by a predecessor body of The United Methodist Church. Its primal identity is Wesleyan Methodist (as in The Wesleyan Church). Only after the Methodist Protestant movement took charge at Adrian (following the Civil War) did the College begin a trajectory toward United Methodist relationship. With that said, Adrian College has been primarily "mainline" in its religious ambience, though recent trends away from denominational loyalty by students are present. This development does not mean Adrian is less religious or Christian. In some respects, there is a renewed willingness to explore traditional conviction, while uniting that with a commitment to social justice.

---

3   Madden and Hamilton, *Freedom and Grace: The Life of Asa Mahan*, 192–221.
4   "Vanderbilt Divinity School, History," https://divinity.vanderbilt.edu/about /history.php.

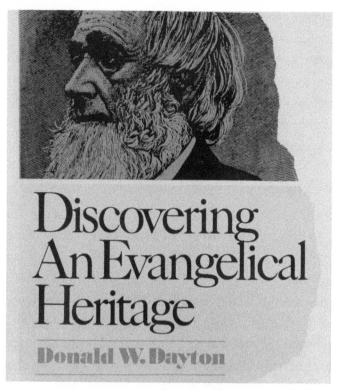

Book cover from Discovering an Evangelical Heritage *by Donald W. Dayton.* © *1976 by Donald Dayton.* Photo by Hollie Smith. Reprinted by permission of HarperCollins Publishers.

The legacy of Asa Mahan cannot be dislocated from the dramatic changes within evangelicalism over the past 150 years. Today many presume that evangelicalism represents a doctrinal purity with little interest in social equality, and there is ample evidence for this presumption. Many of the institutions led by Mahan grew urbane and sophisticated following his death, and they came to express less particular theological ideas. Since the early twentieth century, those committed to evangelical theology have tended to write off places like Oberlin and perhaps even Adrian as wayward children. Newer colleges have claimed Mahan as inspiration; though they seldom, if ever, match his astute and unremitting passion for equality. Today few, if any, embody Mahan's seamless uniting of evangelical theology and unconditional justice.

Adrian College students Mariah Ellison and Jordyn Stone embody Mahan at a program of the Adrian College student antitrafficking organization. Photo by the author. Used with permission.

This state of things was perhaps best confronted in 1976 when Donald W. Dayton asked why the evangelical tradition turned away from social justice. His book, *Discovering an Evangelical Heritage*, served as an indictment of both conservative evangelicalism and self-righteous Protestant liberalism. It is especially noteworthy that the cover of this book's first edition featured the image of Asa Mahan. In 2014 a second edition of the book, under the title: *Rediscovering an Evangelical Heritage: A Tradition and Trajectory of Integrating Piety and Justice*, was released by Professor Dayton and Douglas M. Strong.[5]

---

5   Donald W. Dayton, *Discovering an Evangelical Heritage* (New York: Harper & Row, Publishers, 1976). Donald W. Dayton and Douglas M. Strong, *Rediscovering an Evangelical Heritage: A Tradition and Trajectory of Integrating Piety and Justice* (Grand Rapids, Michigan: Baker Academic, 2014).

Some of us are unwilling to let the possibilities for an integrated witness go. We at least try to be less interested in forcing Mahan's legacy through our preconceived historiographies (left or right). We aspire to learn from him. This is a venture with mixed blessings, given the unavoidable proclivities of different interpretive approaches, but the endeavor does have its rewards.

At Adrian College Asa Mahan's legacy has particular resonance among undergraduate students. "Experts" will tell us that young adults do not care about old, dusty historical figures and their principles, but this is not so. Something about a real, flawed, eccentric old-timer who honestly loved each and all is compelling. I often see students sporting T-shirts with a sketch of Mahan's face on the front and his words, "Intrinsic Worth," on the back. This commitment to inherent dignity is particularly meaningful for those coming of age in a world that measures them by manipulative calculations.

An even more disturbing reality makes Mahan relevant today. For a few decades now, human rights advocates have drawn our attention to the abuse of human trafficking—a commodification of people that is really slavery. Various international organizations estimate that as many as twenty-seven million people are held in bondage throughout the world right now. At Adrian a sizeable number of our deepest students have been working to combat this abuse for over ten years. They have raised funds to help schools in Thailand, have held forums regarding state laws and legal remedies, and have presented to nationally acclaimed academic conferences. When people ask them what organization they represent, they seem unconcerned about name recognition or brands. They are simply being daughters and sons of Asa. That may be the strongest testimony in support of Mahan's continuing impact.

INDEX

Note: Page numbers in italics indicate illustrations.

revivalism, 108; Finney and, 111, 125, 127–28; Mahan and, 137, 159–60, 200. *See also* evangelicals
Revolutionary War, 22–23, 55, 58
Richardson, John, 42
"rightarianism," 118–20, 122
Rollin, Frances Ann, 192n60
Rowe, Henry K., 142–43

Salovey, Peter, 56, 57
sanctification. *See* Holiness
Sandburg, Carl, 24
Sanders, Bernie, 172, 177
Schelling, Friedrich Wilhelm Joseph, 105
Scott, John, 197
Scottish intuitionism, 115
Scottish Realism, 10–14, 38–43, 68, 103; Archibald Alexander and, 84; Frederick Douglass and, 40; Reid and, 37–39; John Witherspoon and, 78. *See also* Enlightenment philosophy
Semple, J. W., 13, 45–47
Seward, William H., 104, 168
Shipherd, John J., 17n1, 111
slave trade, 66–67, 189, 201–2
slavery, 20, 94; Archibald Alexander on, 83, 86–88; John C. Calhoun on, 99; Constitution and, 6–8, 177–92, 202; Thomas Cooper on, 70; David Brion Davis on, 9–10; Jonathan Edwards and, 50–51, 54; Joseph Haven on, 106–7; Samuel Hopkins on, 55–56; human trafficking as, *205,* 206; indentured servants and, 59; Methodist Episcopal Church on, 72–73; Theodore Parker on, 100–101; William Andrew Smith on, 72–74; Francis Wayland on, 88–89, 91–92; John Witherspoon on, 81–82, 88. *See also* abolitionism; emancipation

Smith, Christian, 130
Smith, Gerrit, 174, 185
Smith, James McCune, 40
Smith, William Andrew, 71–75
Spooner, Lysander, 185–87, 189–90
Stanton, Edwin, 197
Stephen, Caroline Emelia, 92–93
Stewart, Dugald, 11–12, 37, 39
Stiles, Ezra, 58–61, 107
Stoddard, Solomon, 48
Stone, Lucy, 132
Streeter, Sereno Wright, 137–38, 142
Strong, Douglas M., 205
Stuart, Moses, 145

Tappan, Arthur, 129
Tappan, Lewis, 111, 128–29
Tawney, R. H., 28
Taylor, Nathaniel William, 64–67, 142
teleology, 55–56; deontology and, 8–9, 31–32, 35, 49, 118–19
Thirteenth Amendment to Constitution, 9, 225–26
Thoreau, Henry David, 35
Torrey, Charles Turner, 103–4
Transcendentalism, 6, 109–14; Coleridge and, 127; Cousin and, 129; Kant and, 12, 111–14
Trinitarianism, 103

Underground Railroad, 190; Coffins and, 106–7; Luther Lee and, 117; Mahan and, 3, 17, 148; Reed and, 195. *See also* abolitionism
Unitarians, 97, 142
United Methodist Church, 203–4. *See also* Wesleyan Methodists
utilitarianism, 8–9, 75; benevolence and, 48; consequentialism and, 97; Finney and, 117, 118, 123, 125; Paley on, 32–33, 35, 36; Parker on, 99; slavery and,

CPSIA information can be obtained
at www.ICGtesting.com
Printed in the USA
LVHW01s1352110918
589745LV00001B/12/P